THE POCKET GUIDE TO
MAMMALS
OF
BRITAIN & EUROPE

THE POCKET GUIDE TO
MAMMALS
OF
BRITAIN & EUROPE

A.M. HUTSON

DRAGON'S WORLD

Dragon's World Ltd
Limpsfield
Surrey RH8 0DY
Great Britain

First published by Dragon's World Ltd, 1995
© Dragon's World 1995
© Text A.M. Hutson, 1995
© Species illustrations individual artists, 1995

Species illustrations by Joanna Brooker, Jim Channell, Sean
Milne and Julia Pewsey.

Editor	Diana Briscoe
Designer	'Designers'
Art Director	John Strange
Design Assistants	Karen Ferguson
	Victoria Furbisher
DTP Manager	Simon Albrow
Editorial Director	Pippa Rubinstein

British Library Cataloguing in Publication Data
The catalogue record for this book is available from the British
Library.

ISBN 1 85028 224 2

Typeset by 'Designers' in Plantin.
Printed in Spain

Contents

Introduction

Over 200 species of mammal occur in Europe, out of a world list of about 4,000 species. Some are quite distinct and easy to see, while others are extremely secretive. Some are so similar to other species that their separation is the sole provenance of specialists. Some species are widespread with their range extending well outside Europe; a few are restricted to a limited area within Europe. This guide shows most of these species and aims to help identify the distinctive species and to make clear where recourse to more detailed literature or experts is required.

Mammals are a diverse group, fully occupying the wide range of habitats available in Europe, from the Arctic tundra and alpine zones through evergreen and deciduous woodland to grasslands and the drier, more open Mediterranean scrub. The mammal fauna of Europe is heavily influenced by humans, not just through their management of its land and waters, but also through the introduction of many species for pleasure, sport, or by accident. This is reflected in the decline of many species and in the growth of others. It is only comparatively recently that interest, and development of study techniques, have allowed observation, research and the identification of conservation needs to match the earlier interests in mammals as pests, quarry animals or as providers of raw materials such as fur and oil.

Identifying Mammals

Many groups of mammals present testing identification problems. Different characters are used for different groups of mammals, so it is important to be aware of the features that are used for identification in each group of mammals. In the field, gait, stance or other behavioural aspects may be characteristic, but difficult to define. Colour patterns combined with shape and size may be distinctive, but these may vary and the relative proportions and detail of some parts will be more important .

In the hand, more detailed features of teeth and relative size and shape of other features can be important, particularly in the smaller animals, and a hand lens and ruler (or, better, calipers) may be necessary. To examine the smaller mammals in the hand it is advisable to have some training to avoid damage to the animal and to avoid being bitten by it.

In particular it is important to be able to recognise the different teeth of many mammals, with the canines or 'dog' teeth usually being the most distinctive and the incisors in front of them and the premolars and then molars behind. The number of each type of tooth in the upper and lower jaws gives the dental formula, which gives general information on the kind of animal being examined, while more detailed examination provides characters for confirming species identification.

In recent years great advances have been made in the interpretation of the high frequency echolocation calls of bats and the ready availability of a range of low cost 'bat detectors' allow the field identification of some species with practice.

For some groups of species, particularly among the rodents and insectivores, reliable identification is not possible in the field, but for the most part the different species of such species-complexes are separated geographically.

Finding and Observing Mammals
Most mammals are nocturnal and secretive, but careful fieldwork will reveal many species and some species may be encountered by chance. Sounds may be identifiable or draw attention to their presence. Binoculars will be useful for the more diurnal mammals of open countryside and water. Careful field observation can allow the watching of a range of ungulates, some carnivores, rodents and lagomorphs, as well as seals. Other artificial aids, such as spotlights or ultrasonic receivers ('bat detectors'), are useful for night use. Cetaceans can be seen from the beach or found stranded on it, but there are also organized whale-watching cruises at appropriate times of year.

Live-trapping of small ground-dwelling species is a widely used method of obtaining information on them, but requires some experience. The search for small mammals may involve disturbance to their habitat, which should always be replaced as found. Trapping and other risk of disturbance should always follow appropriate codes of practice and may require licensing.

Most mammals leave evidence of their presence, such as tracks, footprints, droppings, smell, hair caught on thorns, food remains or the nature of dens and nests. Indeed, often such signs are the first indication of a species being present. Remains of many small mammals may be found in the pellets, droppings or rejected material of larger predatory birds or mammals.

Conserving Mammals
The conservation of Europe's native mammals has become of increasing concern. Some species now only maintain the barest toehold in Europe, although some, such as the beaver, have been brought back successfully from that status. However, in the case of the beaver there was a good basis of knowledge, understanding and enthusiasm, while for some of the smaller, more obscure species too many of those factors may be missing.

Larger species, such as many carnivores, now exist only as relict populations. Some species only remain through captive breeding programmes or reintroduction. Particular habitats, such as woodland, grassland, waterways and caves, are under particular threat and may affect a variety of species. Pollution, development, disturbance, exploitation, even prejudice, can all add to natural catastrophes to endanger species recovery.

National legislation often helps and is augmented by international Directives, Conventions, Agreements and Action Plans. These frequently prioritize species of concern and hence help to concentrate resources where they are most needed. While there have been significant recovery programmes for a few species, different groups face different pressures and each problem requires appropriate research. Increasingly, good population data is required of conservationists as a basis for conservation action, and the surveying and monitoring of mammal species is an area to which anybody can contribute.

Map of Europe showing climate and vegetation shifts from tundra to sub-tropical

Organizations

The Mammal Society
15 Cloisters Business Centre, 8 Battersea Park Road,
London SW8 4BG

The Bat Conservation Trust
The London Ecology Centre, 45 Shelton Street
London WC2H 9HJ

Whale & Dolphin Conservation Society
Alexander House, James Street West, Bath, Avon BA1 2BT

The British Deer Society
Beale Centre, Lower Basildon, Reading, Berks RG8 9NH

World Wide Fund for Nature
Panda House, Weyside Park, Godalming, Surrey GU7 1XR

The **Societas Europaea Mammalogica** is preparing an atlas
of European mammals (on a 50 kilometre grid) and is
expecting to be open for membership in due course.
It can be contacted through: Dr. A.J. Mitchell-Jones
English Nature, Northminster House, Peterborough, PE1 1UA

There is a number of other specialist groups or organizations
for such mammals as hedgehog, rodents, badger, otter, seals
and ungulates.

Further Reading

General publications
Bang, P. & Dahlstrom, P. 1974. *Animal tracks and signs.*
    Collins, London.
Bright, P. 1991. *Where to watch mammals in Britain.* Occasional
    Publication no. 15. Mammal Society, London.
Corbet, G.B. 1978. *The mammals of the Palaearctic Region: a
    taxonomic review.* British Museum (Natural History),
    London. Supplement 1984.
Corbet, G.B. & Harris, S. 1991. *The Handbook of British
    Mammals.* Blackwell Scientific Publications, Oxford.
Corbet, G.B. & Hill, J.E. 1991. *A world list of mammalian species.*
    Natural History Museum Publications, London.
McDonald, D. (ed.) 1984. *The encyclopaedia of mammals.*
    Allen & Unwin, London.

Niethammer, J. & Krapp, F. 1978 et seq. *Handbuch der Saugetiere* Europas. Akad. Verlagsgesellschaft, Wiesbaden. 4 vols published, others in prep.

Nowaki, R.M. 1992. *Walker's mammals of the world.* John Hopkins University Press, Baltimore.

There is a range of national (and European) guides. Book series including a range of mammal species or groups of species are published by Whittet Books and Christopher Helm.

Publications on specific groups of mammals

Ahlen, I. 1990. *The identification of bats in flight.* Swedish Society for the Conservation of Nature / SYAESC, Stockholm.

Bonner, W.N. 1980. *Whales.* Blandford Press, Poole.

Bonner, W.N.1990. *Natural history of seals.* Helm, London.

Churchfield, S. 1990. *Natural history of shrews.* Helm, London.

Corbet, G.B. 1988. The family Erinaceidae: a synthesis of its taxonomy, phylogeny, ecology and zoogeography. *Mammal Review* 18: 117–172.

Evans, P.G.H. 1982. *Guide to the identification of cetaceans in the North East Atlantic.* Mammal Society, London.

Evans, P.G.H. 1987. *The natural history of whales and dolphins.* Helm, London.

Godfrey, G.K. & Crowcroft, P. 1960. *The life of the mole.* Museum Press, London.

Greenaway, F.R. & Hutson, A.M. 1990. *A field guide to British bats.* Coleman, London.

Gurnell, J. 1987. *Natural history of squirrels.* Helm, London.

King, J.E. 1983. *Seals of the world.* British Museum (Natural History), London & University Press, Oxford.

Leatherwood, S. et al. 1983. *Sierra Club handbook of whales and dolphins.* Sierra Club Books, San Francisco.

Mason, I.L. (ed.) 1984. *Evolution of domesticated animals.* Longman, London.

Ransome, R. 1990. *Natural history of hibernating bats.* Helm, London.

Schober, W. & Grimmberger, E. 1987. *Die Fledermause Europas.* Keller, Stuttgart. English translation ed. R.E.Stebbings, 1989, Hamlyn, London.

Stebbings, R.E. 1988. *Conservation of European bats.* Helm, London.

Whitehead, G.K. 1953. *The ancient white cattle of Britain and their descendants.* Faber & Faber, London.

Whitehead, G.K. 1972. *Deer of the world.* Constable, London.

Whitehead, G.K. 1972. *The wild goats of Britain and Ireland.* David & Charles, Devon.

Red-necked Wallaby
Macropus rufogriseus
Marsupialia; Macropodiae

Size head & body 650–900 mm (25.5–35.5 ins);
    tail 650–800 mm (25.5–31.5 ins)
Weight 11–26 kg (24–57 lb)

Identification Typical kangaroo shape with upright stance,
large back legs and long, thick, black-tipped tail. Fur short and
close, grizzled grey-brown above, white-pale grey underneath
with a rusty patch of variable intensity on shoulders.
Range Native to eastern Australia, but animals have escaped
from zoos and established colonies in Britain in Sussex (this
may be extinct), Bedfordshire, Derbyshire and the shores of
Loch Lomond.
Habitat In Britain found in scrubland and adjacent heathland.
Behaviour More or less solitary, but aggregates in good
feeding areas. Most active at dawn and dusk, but also to some
extent at night. Lays up in vegetation or in hollows by day.
Breeding After a thirty-day gestation the single embryo lives
in its mother's belly pouch for about 280 days and then
continues to suckle until twelve to seventeen months old. Peak
birth period in Britain is August to September.
Food In Britain, mainly heather with some grasses, bracken,
bilberry and pine.
Conservation An introduced species, which has relatively little
impact on native European species.
        Similar species None in Europe.

Western Hedgehog
Erinaceus europaeus
Insectivora; Erinaceidae

Size head & body 160–270 mm (6.25–10.75 ins);
     tail 15–40 mm (0.75–1.5 ins)
Weight 1.1–1.6 kg (2.25–3.5 lb)

Identification Compact and spiny with inconspicuous round
ears. Legs partly hidden by long fur on flanks. Face and
underside sparsely clothed in grey-brown, sometimes very
pale fur.
Range In western Europe, west of a line from the north end of
the Adriatic Sea to western Poland, including southern
Scandinavia, Finland and northern Baltic states to about 50°E.
Also on Mediterranean islands except the Balearic islands.
Throughout mainland Britain and Ireland and on most major
islands.

Habitat Deciduous woodland but almost any lowland habitat
up to 2,000 m (6,500 ft) with cover for nesting. Scarce in
coniferous woodland, marshes and moorland.
Behaviour More or less solitary, non-territorial and nocturnal.
Hibernates with frequent arousals in nests of leaves and grass
under scrub, in rabbit burrows and under buildings. Summer
nests less substantial or non-existent.
Breeding Four to six young born mainly in June with second
peak in late summer. Young weaned within four to six weeks.
Food Mainly ground-living invertebrates, occasionally small
vertebrates or their young, carrion, acorns, berries and fungi.
Conservation Not threatened.
Similar species EASTERN HEDGEHOG *E. concolor* of eastern
Europe, Crete and some other Greek islands has a white chest
contrasting with the darker belly.

Algerian or Vagrant Hedgehog
Atelerix algirus

Size head & body 190–250 mm (7.5–9.75 ins);
tail 25–35 mm (1–1.5 ins)
Weight 850 g (30 oz)

Identification Generally much paler than the western
hedgehog, but the latter can be very pale, especially in
Mediterranean areas where both species occur. The Algerian
hedgehog differs from the western hedgehog in having the first
digit of the hind foot much smaller than the rest. Also has a
patterned face, a wider (pencil-width) bare stripe on crown,
more prominent ears and longer legs.
Range From south-western Morocco to Libya, Canary islands,
Balearic islands and Malta. Records of sightings from coastal
France and Spain may be introduced individuals.
Habitat Scrub, plateau grasslands and cultivation, sometimes
in woodland (especially pine), park land and juniper scrub.
Behaviour Does not hibernate and usually nests in burrows.
Breeding Similar to that of the western hedgehog. Young are
weaned at about sixty days.
Food Wide range of invertebrates plus fungi and small
vertebrates including snakes, lizards and frogs.
Conservation Threatened and in need of strict protection.
Similar species LONG-EARED HEDGEHOG *Hemiechinus auritus*
has ears much longer than adjacent spines and there is no
naked stripe on crown. It occurs in Cyprus (*H. a. dorothea*),
Libya and east of the Mediterranean and the Black seas.

Least or Siberian Shrew
Sorex minutissimus
Insectivora; Soricidae

Size head & body 35–50 mm (1.4–2 ins);
   tail 20–30 mm (0.75–1.25 ins)
Weight 1.5–4 g (0.05–0.1 oz)

Identification Very small, with relatively short hind feet (less than 9 mm [0.35 ins]) and short, bare tail. Fur is grey-brown above and pale below. Teeth are red-tipped and those behind front incisors are small and blunt, decreasing evenly in size.
Range In the CIS to eastern Siberia and south to Sichuan in China and parts of Japan. In the west of range has scattered distribution in central and southern Norway, northern Sweden, Finland and Estonia.

Habitat Taiga (wet coniferous forest), swamp edges in deciduous forest, mossy cover in coniferous forest; also in dry pine heaths and other open sandy country.
Behaviour Has many ten to fifteen-minute rests during an otherwise very active life.
Breeding Two litters of three to six young in May to June.
Food Presumably a wide range of invertebrates.
Conservation Unknown status.
Similar species PYGMY WHITE-TOOTHED SHREW *Suncus etruscus* is of similar size, but does not have red-tipped teeth and has quite a different distribution.

Eurasian Pygmy Shrew
Sorex minutus

Size head & body 45–60 mm (1.75–2.5 ins);
  tail 30–45 mm (1.25–1.75 ins)
Weight 2.5–6 g (0.1–0.25 oz)

Identification Fur is dark or mid-brown above and on flanks,
and dirty-white or yellow-grey below. Tail relatively long
(about 70 per cent of head and body length) and thick
compared with common shrew. The third tooth behind front
upper incisor is larger than the second.
Range Widespread in much of Europe, except extreme north
of Scandinavia, and parts of Mediterranean zone. Throughout
British Isles including Ireland and many offshore islands, but
not Shetland, Isles of Scilly and Channel islands.
Habitat Almost anywhere with good ground cover.
Behaviour Solitary, aggressive, active in short busts day and
night. Often uses burrows and runways of other small
mammals, but also makes own tunnels in grass and moss.
Spends more time on surface than common shrew. Climbs and
swims well. Spherical nests of moss, grass or wood shavings
made in ground hollows, fallen trees or clumps of rush or grass.
Breeding Mates April to October. Usually at least two litters
of two to nine young, weaned at about twenty-two days old.
Food Wide range of invertebrates, mostly 2–10 mm
(0.08–0.4 ins) long, and small amounts of plant material.
Conservation Not threatened.
Similar species Other red-toothed shrews *Sorex* species.

Laxmann's Shrew
Sorex caecutiens

Size head & body 50–70 mm (2–2.75 ins);
    tail 31–46 mm (1.25–1.75 ins)
Weight 3.5–7.5 g (0.1–0.25 oz)

Identification Very dark grey-brown above with clearly
demarcated pale, almost white underside and white feet. Tail
about 70 per cent of head and body length. Suggestion of tuft
at tail tip, but not as well marked as tuft found in juveniles of
most other species of this genus. Three teeth behind front
incisor equal in size and evenly spaced.

Range Taiga and tundra zones of northern Sweden, Finland
and around the Baltic states to eastern Poland. To the east,
throughout Siberia to Pacific seaboard and in most of Japan as
well as south to central Mongolia and Korea.
Habitat Coniferous woodland, scrubby river banks in tundra,
and wooded steppes.
Behaviour Active day and night with brief resting periods.
Breeding One or two litters of two to eleven young in spring
or summer. Young probably breed in following year.
Food Similar to common shrew.
Conservation Unknown status.
Similar species Eurasian common shrew *Sorex araneus*.

Eurasian Common Shrew
Sorex araneus

Size head & body 50–85 mm (2–3.5 ins);
  tail 25–45mm (0.9–1.75 ins)
Weight 5–14 g (0.25–0.5 oz)

Identification Tail 50–60 per cent of head and body length.
Fur short, dense, dark grey-brown above, paler brown or
reddish on flanks and pale grey-white beneath. Tail and ears
sometimes white-tipped. Two teeth behind front incisor more
or less equal in size and larger than the third.
Range Widely distributed in northern and eastern Europe to
northern borders of the Black Sea and across to Siberia.
Absent from Ireland and replaced by closely related species in
much of south-western and Mediterranean Europe.
Habitat Anywhere with low cover, to 2,200 m (7,150 ft) in
Tatras mountains. Most frequent in rough grass, scrub,
deciduous woodland, but also in marshes, dunes and heaths.
Behaviour Solitary, aggressive, active day and night in ten
more or less equal bouts. Makes network of runways through
ground vegetation, climbs and swims. Rounded nest of dry
grass and leaves underground or under dense cover. Breeding
nests are larger and domed.
Breeding Season April to September, and two to four litters of
one to ten young weaned at twenty-four days.
Food Great range of invertebrates, occasionally carrion and
small amounts of plant material. May cache food.
Conservation Not threatened.
Similar species In many parts of Europe *S. araneus* is
replaced by other species only separable by details of skull or
chromosomes: FRENCH or MILLET'S SHREW *S. coronatus* occurs
in Jersey and from western Netherlands to the extreme north of
Iberia, north-west Italy and into parts of Germany, Switzerland
and Austria; the SPANISH SHREW *S. granarius* occurs in
mountains of central Spain; APPENNINE SHREW *S. samniticus* is
found in central and
southern
Italy.

Dusky Shrew
Sorex isodon

Size head & body 60–80 mm (2.5–3 ins);
 tail 41–55 mm (1.5–2.25 ins)
Weight 6.5–14.5 g (0.25–0.5 oz)

Identification Sometimes called *S. sinalis*. About the size of
the common shrew, but with very dark, dull-coloured fur on
the back, grading with little demarcation to dingy grey-brown
fur on the underside. Tail more than 70 per cent of head and
body length, but distinctly less than combined head and body.
Feet yellowish and front feet are markedly broad. The five
simple teeth behind the upper incisor decrease uniformly in
size.
Range South-eastern Norway and Finland with wide
distribution eastwards to eastern Siberia and Japan and
southwards to Shensi in China.
Habitat Wet coniferous forest.
Behaviour Poorly known.
Breeding Poorly known.
Food Not recorded.
Conservation Presumably not threatened.
Similar species Eurasian Common Shrew *S. araneus* (see
page 17).

Alpine Shrew
Sorex alpinus

Size head & body 60–80 mm (2.5–3 ins);
        tail 55–75 mm (2.25–3 ins)
Weight 5.5–13 g (0.25–0.5 oz)

Identification Largest European *Sorex* species, and very
distinctive with dark grey fur, only slightly paler underneath.
Tail about length of head and body, clothed in short hairs, dark
above and very pale, distinctly whitish underneath. Feet
whitish, and five small pads on underside of front foot.
The fourth and fifth simple teeth behind front incisor are of
equal size.

Range Mountains, generally between 600 and 3,000 m
(2,000–9,750 ft): small part of Pyrenees and more widely in
central and eastern Europe, from Jura, Harz and northern Italy
in the west to the Balkans in the south-east and up through the
Tatras and Carpathians to the Sudetan mountains in the north.
Records from the Pyrenees may be suspect.
Habitat Moist montane forests, especially near water. Also
streamsides in alpine meadows and moorland.
Behaviour Little known.
Breeding One or two litters of about six young in summer.
Food Not recorded.
Conservation Not threatened.
Similar species Dark underside and distribution distinctive.

Eurasian Water Shrew
Neomys fodiens

Size head & body 67–96 mm (2.5–3.75 ins);
 tail 45–80 mm (1.75–3 ins)
Weight 10–20 g (0.25–0.75 oz)

Identification Large, slaty-black fur above, sharply
demarcated from silvery-grey fur beneath. Sometimes
underside darker and sometimes a slight, dirty yellow-brown
mid-ventral line. Tail nearly as long as head and body, dark
brown above and white below with a mid-ventral keel of stiff
hairs. Sometimes a tuft of white hairs on small, largely
concealed ears. Feet fringed with stiff silver hairs, and upper
surface of hind feet covered with white hairs. Teeth red-tipped,
but only four simple teeth behind the incisor.

Range Widely distributed from arctic Scandinavia to
mountains of Mediterranean zone (to about 2,000 m [6,500
ft]) and east to Siberia. Absent from most of Iberia and the
Balkans, Ireland and many smaller islands in Britain.
Habitat Banks of well-vegetated, clear, fast-flowing,
unpolluted waterways, also ponds, lakes and ditches.
Sometimes on rocky beaches or far from water.
Behaviour Solitary, probably mildly territorial. Particularly
active at night, strongly aquatic. Burrows in banks, or uses
burrows of voles and mice. Nests of moss, leaves or grass, bark
or roots.
Breeding From April to September, with two or three litters of
3–15 (usually 6–7), which leave the nest at about twenty-four
days, but stay with mother until about forty days old.
Food Invertebrates, mainly freshwater crustaceans and caddis;
occasional small fish, frogs, newts. Prey may be cached.
Similar species Southern Water Shrew *N. anomalus.*

Southern Water Shrew
Neomys anomalus

Size head & body 64–88 mm (2.5–3.5 ins);
      tail 42–67 mm (1.75–2.75 ins)
Weight 7.5–17 g (0.25–0.5 oz)

Identification Similar to Eurasian water shrew, but more consistently pale on underside. Tail also bicoloured, but keel of stiff hairs absent or slight and only on distal third. Fringes of hair on feet less well developed.
Range Fragmented distribution in montane woodland of west and central Europe: Spain, Massif Central of France, Alps, Italy, Germany, Belgium, Poland, the Balkans and eastwards including north-eastern Turkey to the Crimea. Distribution more continuous in eastern Europe where it occupies a greater range of altitude.
Habitat Swamps, damp grassland within montane woodland, streamsides.
Behaviour Active day and night, but activity concentrated into two peaks. Less aquatic than Eurasian water shrew.
Breeding Mating starts in May and there are two litters of five to twelve young.
Food Similar to Eurasian water shrew.
Similar species Eurasian Water Shrew *N. fodiens*.

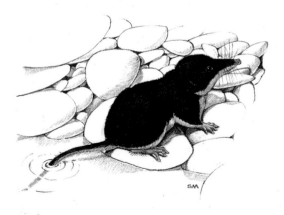

Lesser White-toothed Shrew
Crocidura suaveolens

Size head & body 50–80 mm (2–3 ins);
    tail 24–44 mm (1–1.75 ins)
Weight 3–7 g (0.1–0.25 oz).

Identification Dark greyish or reddish brown above, slightly paler, sometimes yellowish below. Tail more than half the length of head and body, and with sparse, long hairs. Hind feet covered with whitish hairs. Teeth more or less white and second upper simple tooth distinctly smaller than third.
Range Coastal Iberia and France, through Mediterranean Europe (including many islands) to western Turkey. Absent from most of eastern Iberia and France, but is found in northern to central France and more widely in eastern Europe north to southern Poland. In British Isles, only on Isles of Scilly and Sark and Jersey in Channel islands.
Habitat Temperate woodland and steppes: on Isles of Scilly among boulders, rotting seaweed and strand vegetation; coastal dunes, scrub and heath in Jersey; maquis in France; fields, orchards and gardens in Poland.
Behaviour Solitary but not territorial. Principally nocturnal. Excavates burrows, uses runways of other animals and tunnels through humus and litter layer. Spherical nest of tightly woven grass and twigs with roof and several entrances.
Breeding Breeds March to September with about three or four litters of one to six (usually three) young. From about eight days family will 'caravan' if nest disturbed.
Food Wide range of arthropods, fresh carrion, grain.
Similar species Other white-toothed shrews, *Crocidura* species.

Greater White-toothed Shrew
Crocidura russula

Size head & body 60–90 mm (2.5–3.5 ins);
tail 33–60 mm (1.25–2.5 ins)
Weight 4.5–14.5 g (0.25–0.5 oz)

Identification Very similar to but larger than white-toothed shrew, with upper fur greyish to reddish brown with no clear demarcation from duller yellowish grey underparts. The second simple tooth in upper jaw is only slightly smaller than the third.

Range Southern and central western Europe from Netherlands to central Germany and south to French/Italian border. Also on Sardinia, some other Mediterranean islands and North Africa. Usually below 1,000 m (3,250 ft).
Habitat Woodland, hedgerows, maquis, dry grassland, cultivations, particularly around buildings. Often in dry-stone walls.
Behaviour Solitary, not territorial. Active day and night, but more diurnal than lesser white-toothed shrew. Nest of dry grass and leaves under cover has no roof.
Breeding Can extend from February to October with several litters of two to eleven (usually four). 'Caravanning' occurs from about seven days and young are weaned at about twenty-five days.
Food Wide range of invertebrates with occasional young of lizards and small rodents and sometimes plant material.
Conservation Unknown status.
Similar species Populations to the east (southern Poland, Czechoslovakia, Romania and Bulgaria) are now regarded as a distinct species, *C. gueldenstaedtii*. Sicilian population sometimes separated as *C. sicula*.

Bicoloured White-toothed Shrew

Crocidura leucodon

Size head & body 64–90 mm (2.5–3.5 ins);
     tail 28–40 mm (1–1.5 ins)
Weight 6–15 g (0.25–0.5 oz)

Identification Dark brown upper parts clearly demarcated from grey-white underparts. Tail relatively short, about half body length, and bicoloured. Third simple tooth behind upper incisor is distinctly smaller than second.
Range From northern and eastern France through central Europe and southern CIS to the River Volga, the Caucasus and perhaps to Asia Minor and Palestine. Absent from most Mediterranean peninsulas and islands.
Habitat Dry lowlands, including deciduous woodland edges, scrub, arable fields, meadows and gardens, often near and in human habitation. Less common in more open habitats than greater white-toothed shrew.
Behaviour Active day and night but perhaps more nocturnal than related species. Domed nest of fresh or dry grass with one side entrance in shelter.
Breeding Mates between April and October; gestation about thirty days; two to four litters of three to six young, independent in three to four weeks.
Food Range of invertebrates, occasional small rodent, plant material and raids human's larders.
Conservation Status unknown.
Similar species *C. lasia* and/or *C. zimmermanni* from parts of Asia Minor including Crete, Lesbos and other Aegean islands.

Pygmy White-toothed Shrew
Suncus etruscus

Size head & body 35–50 mm (1.5–2 ins);
     tail 24–30 mm (1–1.25 ins)
Weight 1.5–2 g (0.05–0.07 oz)

Identification Smallest European mammal and perhaps the smallest in the world. Ears relatively large and tail relatively long. Dull reddish or grey-brown above, slightly paler below. Tail black-brown above and paler below. Whole animal, including tail, covered with sparse long hairs. Teeth white and four simple teeth in upper jaw.

Range Lowland coastal Mediterranean zone from Spain to Greece including most islands: Majorca, Sardinia, Corsica, Sicily, Crete and Corfu. Atlantic coast of southern Portugal and France. Patchy distribution in northern and western Africa and east to about 80°E in India and Sri Lanka.
Habitat Sunny, open terrain, especially cork oak woodland, grassland, hedgerow, scrub and gardens, up to over 600 m (2,000 ft) in France and 1,000 m (3,250 ft) in Italy.
Behaviour Builds nests under stones, logs, among tree roots or in ground cavities. Active on and off throughout the twenty-four-hour day.
Breeding Five to six litters of two to six young.
Food Range of insects up to size of grasshoppers and crickets.

Pyrenean Desman

Galemys pyrenaicus
Insectivora; Talpidae

Size head & body 110–135 mm (4.5–5.25 ins);
    tail: 130–155 mm (5–6 ins)
Weight 50–80 g (2–3 oz)

Identification Muzzle very long, flattened, spatulate and mobile with valved nostrils at tip. Eyes small, neck short. Fringe of stiff bristles on all feet, especially hind feet, which are large and webbed. Tail long, constricted at the base where there are powerful musk glands, flattened laterally towards tip, which is fringed with long hairs. Glossy dark brown above, silvery-white underneath, often with a yellowish breast patch.
Range Patchy distribution in Pyrenees and other mountains of north-west Spain and northern Portugal.
Habitat Fast-flowing waterways bordered by deciduous vegetation. From 300 m (1,000 ft) to 2,000 m (6,500 ft).
Behaviour Very active and agile, swims and dives well. Solitary, nocturnal. Nests in holes in banks, under tree roots and rocks.
Breeding Mates from January to February, litters of two to four young born from March to July.
Food Aquatic invertebrates and occasional small vertebrates.
Conservation Requires unpolluted and unshaded water, so afforestation and pollution have caused sharp declines and fragmented populations.
Similar species RUSSIAN DESMAN *Desmana moschata* is similar, but 220 mm (8.5 ins) long. Found in south-western Russia in Don and Volga and has been introduced to other rivers near European border.

European Mole
Talpa europea

Size head & body 110–150 mm (4.25–6 ins);
   tail 25–50 mm (1–2 ins)
Weight 75–125 g (3–4 oz)

Identification Velvety black fur, spade-like forelimbs with
very large claws and simple hindlimbs. Tail short and
constricted at base. Pointed, pink, fleshy snout with sensory
vibrissae; no external ear; small eyes; no apparent neck.
Range: Most of Europe east to central Siberia. Throughout
mainland Britain and many islands, but absent from Ireland.
Absent from northern Scandinavia and Finland, much of
Iberia, Italy and parts of the Balkans.

Habitat Deciduous woodland but also pasture and arable land
and occurs up to 2,000 m (6,500 ft) in Alps.
Behaviour Solitary and territorial, mostly in extensive tunnel
system often indicated by surface mounds. Excavates large nest
chambers lined with dry grass or leaves. Active for about three
periods of three to four hours per day. Young moles spend
some time on surface before establishing own tunnels.
Breeding Mates in April and early summer; gestation about
four weeks; single litter (occasionally two) of three to four
young born from April to July, weaned at about five weeks.
Food Invertebrates, mainly earthworms, that drop into tunnels
and also scavenge on surface. Mutilate heads of prey and
cache.
Conservation Heavily persecuted in parts of range.
Similar species In the south replaced by Mediterranean Mole
T. caeca (see page 28).

Mediterranean Mole
Talpa caeca

Size head & body 100–130 mm (4–5 ins);
tail 25–37 mm (1–1.5 ins)
Weight 40–65 g (1.75–2.75 oz)

Identification Smaller than the European mole. Eyes are permanently covered by a membrane. Nose vibrissae and hairs of legs and tail paler than in European mole. Inner upper incisors more than twice the size of outer incisors (less than twice in European mole).
Range Mainland of Mediterranean region south of Alps in south-east France, northern Italy, southern Switzerland, former Yugoslavia and Greece. Also Asia Minor.

Habitat As far as is known similar to European mole.
Behaviour As far as is known similar to European mole.
Breeding As far as is known similar to European mole.
Food As far as is known similar to European mole.
Conservation As far as is known similar to European mole.
Similar species Mole classification is currently under scrutiny. SPANISH MOLE *T. occidentalis* is one currently recognized as a closely-related species; smaller than the Northern or European mole (see page 27), and found in the mountains of Spain to about 2,300 m (7,500 ft), but not in the north-east nor the Pyrenees. Populations in northern Italy have been described as a separate subspecies *T. c. augustana*.

Roman Mole
Talpa romana

Size head & body 125–165 mm (5–6.5 ins);
tail 24–40 mm (1–1.5 ins)
Weight 60–100 g (2.25–4 oz)

Identification Larger and with broader muzzle than
European mole; eyes permanently covered by a membrane.
Range Below 2,300 m (7,500 ft) in southern Italy (including
Sicily), southern France and Greece.
Habitat As other moles.
Behaviour As other moles.
Breeding As other moles.
Food Earthworms, slugs, beetles, leatherjackets.
Similar species Moles in southern former Yugoslavia,
northern Greece and Corfu are frequently considered as a
separate species: the BALKAN MOLE *T. stankovici.*

Egyptian Fruit Bat

Rousettus aegypticus
Chiroptera, Pteropodidae

Size head & body 130–150 mm (5–6 ins);
forearm 85–102 mm (3.25–4 ins)
Weight 90–170 g (3.5–6 oz)

Identification The only European fruit bat, with typical large eyes and dog-like face. The base of the ear forms a complete ring. The fur is almost plain grey, often reddish in Africa, with a paler collar and light belly fur.

Range Eastern Mediterranean to Pakistan and throughout Africa south of the Sahara, also on Cyprus and south coast of Turkey.

Habitat In areas with fruit trees and cave-like roost sites.

Behaviour Colonial and nocturnal. Roosts in caves, rock crevices, wells and disused buildings during the day.

Breeding In Eastern Mediterranean two breeding peaks: March to April and August to September, but individuals only have one young per year. Gestation is four months and the mother carries or guards the single young for about six weeks. The young fly at nine to ten weeks and are weaned at three to four months.

Food Soft ripe fruits, especially figs, carob and Persian lilac as well as commercial crops, such as loquats and dates.

Conservation It has increased through commercial fruit growing around the Mediterranean and is persecuted by fruit growers for perceived crop damage.

Similar species None in region.

Greater Horseshoe Bat
Rhinolophus ferrumequinum
Chiroptera, Rhinolophidae

Size head & body 56–71 mm (2–2.75 ins);
forearm 50–61 mm (2–2.5 ins)
Weight 13–34 g (0.5–1.5 oz)

Identification Characteristic horseshoe-shaped dish on nose
(noseleaf); ears have no tragus (inner lobe of ear). The largest
of all the European horseshoe bats.
Range Reduced in Britain to south Wales and south-west
England; south from northern France, central Germany and
southern Czechoslovakia to the Mediterranean and major
islands; western North Africa, Middle East, Caucasus and
fragmented populations across to Japan.
Habitat Open park land, scrub, pasture and wooded slopes,
often near water and caves.
Behaviour Roosts in caves and buildings. Females are colonial
in summer; males and immatures aggregate in winter.
Breeding Mates mostly in autumn. Summer maternity
colonies of up to 200 or more; single young born in late June to
early July. Young independent by seven to eight weeks.
Food Chafers, dung beetles, moths and crane-flies taken in
flight, from perches or from ground. Feeding debris can be
found at feeding perches in tunnels and porches (as with other
horseshoe bat species).
Conservation This bat is now absent from large parts of its
former northern range in Britain, the Netherlands, etc.

Lesser Horseshoe Bat
Rhinolophus hipposideros

Size head & body 35–45 mm (1.25–1.75 ins);
forearm 35–43 mm (1.25–1.75 ins)
Weight 4–9.5 g (0.1–0.25 oz)

Identification The smallest European horseshoe bat.

Range Now found mainly from south-western British Isles, France, Germany and southern Poland south to Mediterranean and islands and into western North Africa. Also Caucasus, Middle East and in scattered populations to about 70°E.

Habitat Lowland sheltered valleys and foothills to about 1,100 m (3,500 ft) close to caves.

Behaviour Summer roosts are in caves or, in the north, in buildings. In winter hibernates in caves, tunnels and cellars in loose clusters or singly.

Breeding Maternity roosts may start to assemble in April and build from ten up to a hundred individuals or more; the single young is born in June to July. Young fly at about three weeks and are independent at six to seven weeks. Colonies disperse between August and October.

Food Range of flies, caddis flies, lacewings and small moths. Also beetles, spiders, bugs and small wasps. Often flies close to ground and gleans prey from stones and branches.

Conservation Absent from much of its former range in northern Europe and is one of the most highly endangered species.

Similar species Other horseshoe bats are larger.

Mediterranean Horseshoe Bat
Rhinolophus euryale

Size head & body 43–58 mm (1.75–2.25 ins);
forearm 42–51 mm (1.75–2 ins)
Weight 8–18 g (0.25–0.75 oz)

Identification Medium-sized horseshoe bat, nose-leaf
narrower than other species. Difficult to separate from
Blasius's and Mehely's horseshoe bats but second phalanx of
fourth finger is more than twice as long as first, and there are
differences in noseleafs. When at roost, wings do not enclose
body to extent seen in other horseshoe bat species.
Range Mediterranean region and Balkans. Occurs north to
southern France, northern Italy and Switzerland, southern
Czechoslovakia. Major Mediterranean islands, western North
Africa, the Middle East and east to about 60°E.
Habitat Well-wooded countryside and scrub close to water
and caves.
Behaviour Usually roosts in caves in summer, but also in
buildings towards northern edge of range. Winter roosts are in
caves and tunnels.
Breeding Similar to other horseshoe bats.
Food Moths and other insects are taken to a regular feeding
perch.
Conservation Restricted
distribution and vulnerable.
Similar species Difficult to
separate from other
horseshoe bat species,
especially Blasius's *R. blasii*
and Mehely's *R. mehelyi* (see
pages 34, 35).

Mehely's Horseshoe Bat
Rhinolophus mehelyi

Size head & body 55–64 mm (2.25–2.5 ins);
forearm 48–55 mm (1.75–2.25 ins)
Weight 10–18 g (0.5–0.75 oz)

Identification A medium-sized bat, generally very pale,
especially underneath, and with more or less distinct darker fur
around eye. Distinguished by differences in noseleaf (shape of
upper pointed 'lancet'), shape of lower face, of process arising
from centre of horseshoe ('sella') and profile of its upper flange
('connecting process').
Range Iberia (except north-east), southern Italy, coastal
former Yugoslavia, Albania, Greece, southern Bulgaria,
Romania, Balearic Islands, Sardinia, Sicily, many eastern
Mediterranean islands. Also western North Africa, Asia Minor
and Caucasus east to Iran.
Habitat Poorly known.
Behaviour Poorly known but presumed similar to their more
widespread relatives. Roosts almost exclusively in caves.
Breeding Poorly known, but breeding colonies may number
up to about 500.
Food Moths and other insects – presumably caught from
feeding perch and taken back there, or to some other spot, for
dismemberment and consumption.
Conservation Poorly known.
Similar species Other horseshoe bats.

Blasius's Horseshoe Bat
Rhinolophus blasii

Size head & body 46–54 mm (1.75–2.25 ins);
forearm 44–50 mm (1.75–2 ins)
Weight 11–16 g (0.5–0.75 oz)

Identification Medium-sized horseshoe bat. The second phalanx of the fourth finger is no more than twice the length of the first. Noseleaf differences.

Range Southern Africa, Ethiopia, western North Africa and then from eastern Mediterranean (including islands), south-west Asia and the Caucasus east to about 70°E. In Europe in coastal north-east Italy and former Yugoslavia, Albania, Greece and southern parts of surrounding countries, including Bulgaria. One doubtful record from Spain.

Habitat Scrub and open woodland close to caves.

Behaviour Little known, but known roosts are all in caves.

Breeding Little known, but breeding colonies may number up to 200.

Food Probably similar to Mediterranean horseshoe bat.

Conservation The rarest and most poorly known of European horseshoe bats.

Similar species Other horseshoe bats, particularly the Mediterranean *R. euryale* (see page 33) and Mehely's *R. mehelyi*.

Whiskered Bat

Myotis mystacinus
Chiroptera, Vespertilionidae

Size head & body 35–48 mm (1.5–1.75 ins);
    forearm 31–37 mm (1.25–1.5 ins)
Weight 4–8 g (0.1–0.25 oz)

Identification The ears of bats of the genus *Myotis* are
separate at the base, and the tragus (inner lobe of ear) is
elongate and more or less pointed. This is the smallest *Myotis*,
and the hair has distinctive bronze tips. The margin of the tail
has no obvious fringe of hairs. Difficult to separate from
Brandt's bat; the penis is narrow and parallel-sided in this

species and the tragus is more pointed. Second upper premolar
distinctly smaller than first.
Range Widespread but nowhere common. Throughout British
Isles, except much of Scotland. From 65°N in Scandinavia,
south to Mediterranean and its islands and Morocco. East to
Pacific and Japan. Absent from much of Iberia.
Habitat Woodland edges and tracks, parks and gardens, often
near water.
Behaviour Very few hibernation sites known; in the caves and
tunnels where it has been found, it is often found close to
entrances hanging free.
Breeding Summer breeding colonies of about seventy
individuals in crevices around buildings, in trees and tunnels.
Single young.
Food Usually feeds at up to 6 m (20 ft) above ground, on
midges, mayflies, moths, small dragonflies, beetles and spiders.
Conservation Threatened.
Similar species Brandt's Bat *M. brandtii.*

Brandt's Bat
Myotis brandtii

Size head & body 38–51 mm (1.5–2 ins);
    forearm 31–39 mm (1.25–1.5 ins)
Weight 4.5–9.5 g (0.1–0.5 oz)

Identification Averages larger than whiskered bat with upper fur more reddish brown. Tragus blunter and penis is bulbous. Second upper premolar is more or less equal in size to first.
Range Difficulty of separating whiskered and Brandt's bats means that distribution is poorly known. Widely recorded in England, Wales and southern Scotland; absent from Ireland. Brandt's recorded from Scandinavia to about 65°N and may extend further north than whiskered bat, but does not extend so far south, reaching only north of Spain, Italy and Greece. Also eastwards from Europe to Kamchatka and Kuril Islands.
Habitat Woodland edges and rides, but feeds more in woodland than whiskered bat.
Behaviour More frequently hibernates in crevices in caves and tunnels.
Breeding Summer maternity colonies of up to sixty in crevices in buildings. Single young.
Food Maybe a more strictly aerial feeder
than whiskered bat.
Conservation Threatened.
Similar species
Whiskered Bat
M. mystacinus.

Geoffroy's Bat
Myotis emarginatus

Size head & body 41–53 mm (1.5–2 ins);
    forearm 36–41 mm (1.25–1.5 ins)
Weight 7–15 g (0.25–0.6 oz)

Identification Distinct notch on outer margin of ear, more marked than in other species, gives it alternative name of notch-eared bat. Rusty red-brown fur above, yellowish below.
Range Central and southern Europe; southern Netherlands, southern and western Germany, southern Poland and south to Mediterranean and Balkans. Also on Sardinia, Corsica, Sicily and Crete. Outside Europe: north-western Africa, the Middle East to Iran, the Crimea and Caucasus to Tashkent.

Habitat Lowlands and foothills to about 1,000 m (3,250 ft), parks and gardens, usually near water.
Behaviour Hangs free in roosts, usually caves but also buildings, often occurring with greater horseshoe bats. Spends winter in relatively warm parts of caves and tunnels.
Breeding Maternity colonies of twenty to 200, but up to 1,000 in Balkans. Single young born mid to late June to early July.
Food Moths and flies, particularly midges; also spiders and caterpillars. Takes prey from vegetation or ground.
Conservation Retreating at northern limits and one of Europe's most endangered species.
Similar species Other *Myotis* species.

Natterer's Bat
Myotis nattereri

Size head & body 40–50 mm (1.5–2 ins);
  forearm 36–43 mm (1.25–1.75 ins)
Weight 6.5–12 g (0.25–0.5 oz)

Identification Ears quite long, curved back at tip and splayed when bat torpid. Tragus very long and narrow. Margin of tail wrinkled by bases of a row of stiff-curved bristles.Calcar (cartilaginous spur from keel) S-shaped giving broad tail. Fur sandy brown above, very white below.
Range Widespread, from southern Sweden, Denmark and Estonia south to Mediterranean except south-east Balkans and islands. Morocco. East through CIS to Japan.
Habitat Woodland edges, open forest, hedgerows, park land and edges of water and marsh.
Behaviour Roosts in tree-holes, bat boxes and buildings in summer. In winter it is common in caves and tunnels, usually in colder sites. Emerges late in evening and flies generally less than 6 m (20 ft) above ground.
Breeding Maternity colonies usually twenty to eighty, sometimes 200. Single young.
Food Flies, moths, caddis flies, beetles and spiders, including many day-flying insects picked from vegetation.
Conservation Threatened.
Similar species Other *Myotis* species.

Bechstein's Bat
Myotis bechsteinii

Size head & body 43–55 mm (1.75–2.25 ins);
    forearm 38–47 mm (1.5–2 ins)
Weight 7–14 g (0.25–0.5 oz)

Identification Extremely long ears, held parallel when the bat
is torpid. No hair or bristle fringe along the margin of the tail.
Bare pink face, sandy to rich brown upper fur, very white
underneath.
Range Widespread, but patchy distribution from southern
Sweden to Portugal, central and northern Spain, Corsica and
Italy. Absent from Baltic and most of Balkans. East to western
Russia and Caucasus. In Britain, only in southern central
England.
Habitat Old mixed woodland; also pine forest, parks and
gardens.
Behaviour Summer roosts mainly in tree-holes, sometimes in
buildings, bat boxes and rock crevices. Scarce in caves and
tunnels in winter so probably in tree-holes. Emerges late (as
most *Myotis* species) and flies low.
Breeding Maternity colonies of ten to thirty change site
frequently. Single young.
Food Moths, beetles, small flies, most taken from vegetation or
ground.
Conservation Decline probably reflects the loss of old mixed
woodland.
Similar species Could be confused with long-eared bats
(*Plecotus* species), but they have ears joined at bases.

Greater Mouse-eared Bat
Myotis myotis

Size head & body 67–80 mm (2.5–3.25 ins);
forearm 54–68 mm (2–2.5 ins)
Weight 25–45 g (1–1.75 oz)

Identification Largest *Myotis* species. Pale brown upper fur,
white below. Broad pink muzzle.
Range Extinct in British Isles; single record in southern
Sweden; absent from most of the Netherlands and northern
Germany. Some healthy populations in Poland, central and
southern Europe, including Mediterranean islands, Balkans to
Middle East and Ukraine.

Habitat Open country with trees, park land, meadow and
pasture.
Behaviour In winter in warmer parts of caves and tunnels,
hanging freely in clusters. Emerges to feed late in evening,
flying at about 10–20 m (32–65 ft), but will also feed from
ground.
Breeding Summer maternity colonies in caves and tunnels, or
in buildings in north of range, may contain up to 2,000 bats.
Young often born in early June.
Food Carabid, chafers and dung beetles, as well as crickets,
grasshoppers, moths and spiders.
Conservation Retreating in northern part of range.
Similar species Very difficult to separate from Lesser Mouse-
eared Bat *M. blythii* (see page 42). All other *Myotis* species are
much smaller.

Lesser Mouse-eared Bat
Myotis blythii

Size head & body 62–71 mm (2.5–2.75 ins);
forearm 50–61 mm (2–2.5 ins)
Weight 15–30 g (0.5–1.25 oz)

Identification Compared with greater mouse-eared bat, ears and tragus are narrower and more delicate and tail is usually longer than forearm but difficult to separate. Often has pale spot on forehead.
Range More southerly than greater mouse-eared, but ranges overlap. Found from Mediterranean north to south-eastern  France, Switzerland, Austria, the Czech Republic, Slovakia and Romania. Isolated records from further north. More widely distributed on Mediterranean islands but absent from Balearics. Also occurs in north-western Africa, Middle East and across CIS to Himalayas and China.
Habitat Open tree and scrub areas, parks and around settlements. Perhaps moves further into drier areas than does its relative.
Behaviour Summer roosts in warm caves, often with Schreiber's bent-winged bats or horseshoe bats, sometimes in attics or tree-holes. Winter roosts in warmer parts of caves and tunnels, mostly hanging free.
Breeding Summer maternity colonies of up to 5,000.
Food Similar to greater mouse-eared bat, but with higher proportion of grasshoppers and crickets.
Conservation Threatened.
Similar species Greater Moused-eared Bat *M. myotis* (see page 41), similar in appearance and often share roosts.

Daubenton's Bat
Myotis daubentonii

Size head & body 45–55 mm (1.75–2.25 ins);
forearm 33–42 mm (1.25–1.75 ins)
Weight 6–15 g (0.25–0.5 oz)

Identification Large feet, more than half the length of shin with long, strong bristles, some reaching beyond claws. Tragus less than half the length of the ear with convex outer edge. Fur uniform red-brown above, dingy white below.
Range From central Finland and Scandinavia to the Mediterranean, Corsica, Sardinia and Italy. Absent from southern France and Balkans. East through central and southern CIS to Korea, Manchuria and Japan.
Habitat In flat, open country, woodland and park land near water.
Behaviour Most summer roosts are in trees, and in winter it is a common species in caves and tunnels. Emerges late and flies fast and generally below 5 m (16 ft). Feeds near water surface, taking small insects from air and by 'gaffing' insects from water surface.
Breeding Maternity roosts may number twenty to sixty, sometimes up to 200.
Food Mainly midges, mayflies, caddis flies and some moths.
Conservation One of the few European bat species that may be increasing in numbers.
Similar species Long-fingered Bat *M. capaccinii* and Pond Bat *M. dasycneme* (see pages 44, 45). The very similar LITTLE BROWN BAT *M. lucifugus* of North America has been recorded in Europe as a result of ship-assisted passage.

Long-fingered Bat
Myotis capaccinii

Size head & body 45–53 mm (1.75–2 ins);
    forearm 38–44 mm (1.5–1.75 ins)
Weight 6–15 g (0.25–0.5 in)

Identification Dorsal fur is dense and woolly, brown with broad, pale-grey or yellowish tips. Dense covering of long fur on the hind legs and adjacent parts of the flight membrane. Large feet (as Daubenton's) with long bristles.
Range From eastern Spain and southern France through Italy to much of the Balkans and on Mediterranean islands: Balearics, Corsica, Sardinia and Sicily. Also in western North Africa and the Middle East to Uzbekistan.

Habitat Prefers caves in woodland and scrub.
Behaviour Uses caves all year round and may be found in crevices under bridges in summer. Emerges late and frequently feeds low over water.
Breeding Maternity colonies of up to 500 females.
Food Small flying insects.
Conservation Nowhere common.
Similar species Daubenton's Bat *M. daubentonii* (see page 43) and Pond Bat *M. dasycneme*.

Pond Bat
Myotis dasycneme

Size head & body 57–67 mm (2.25–2.5 ins);
    forearm 43–50 mm (1.75–2 ins)
Weight 14–20 g (0.5–0.75 oz)

Identification Dense fur, but sleeker than Daubenton's bat
and with a blunt muzzle that gives it a 'bull-headed' look.
Tragus is less than half the length of the ear. Fine white hairs
on lower parts of legs and on underside of tail membrane. Feet
large with long bristles.
Range From northern France and Switzerland to Denmark
and southern Sweden, east to the Baltic states and down to
Austria, Hungary and northern Romania. In the CIS to 48°N
and east to the River Yenisey.
Habitat Rivers, canals and lakes with adjacent meadows and
woodland.
Behaviour Summer roosts are usually in open roof spaces or
sometimes in hollow trees. Hibernates in caves and tunnels, not
usually in clusters. Emerges well after dark and feeds close to
water surface.
Breeding Maternity colonies of up to 400 or more, usually in
large high buildings such as churches.
Food Aquatic insects such as mayflies, stoneflies, midges,
mosquitoes, beetles, moths, crane-flies.
Conservation Significant declines have been recorded and
its restricted habitat requirements and distribution merit the
special attention of conservationists.
Similar species Daubenton's Bat *M. daubentonii* (see page
43) and Long-fingered Bat *M. capaccinii.*

Common Pipistrelle
Pipistrellus pipistrellus

Size head & body 33–51 mm (1.25–2 ins);
       forearm 28–35 mm (1–1.25 ins)
Weight 4–8.5 g (0.1–0.5 oz)

Identification In all *Pipistrellus* species, there is a distinct
post-calcarial lobe of skin, the short ears have rounded tips and
the elongated tragus is curved inwards, but is more or less
parallel-sided and blunt-tipped. In this species, the dense sleek
fur is rufous to chocolate-brown, not clearly demarcated from
paler underside.
Range From about 61°N south to the Mediterranean. Madeira
and all major Mediterranean islands, North Africa and from
the Middle East to Afghanistan. Throughout British Isles and
most major offshore islands including Orkney.

Habitat Woodland edges, hedgerows, parks and gardens
including those in major cities. Often near water.
Behaviour Summer roosts are in tree holes and fissures or
around outside of buildings. Winter roosts are recorded in
buildings, trees, caves, tunnels and rock crevices; emerges to
feed when temperature exceeds 10°C.
Breeding Maternity colonies often number up to 200 and can
reach 1,000 for short periods. Males hold autumn mating
territories.
Food Small flies, mayflies, caddis flies, lacewings and moths.
Conservation Not threatened but like many bat species is
declining in parts of range.
Similar species Nathusius's Pipistrelle *P. nathusii*.

Nathusius's Pipistrelle
Pipistrellus nathusii

Size head & body 46–55 mm (1.75–2.25 ins);
forearm 31–37 mm (1.25–1.5 ins)
Weight 6–15 g (0.25–0.5 oz)

Identification Similar to common pipistrelle, but larger and with longer fur. Ratio of fifth finger to forearm usually more than 1.25, and length of fifth digit including width of wrist more than 42 mm (1.65 ins); less in common pipistrelle. Unlike common pipistrelle, first upper premolar clearly visible and a distinct gap between outer lower incisors.
Range Most of northern Europe from southern Sweden, Finland and the Baltic states, migrating to the Mediterranean and Corsica. Absent from most of south-western France and Iberia. An occasional winter migrant to Britain. East to the Urals and the Caucasus.
Habitat Edges of rides of deciduous and coniferous woodland and park land, often near water and human habitation.
Behaviour Summer roosts are in tree holes and fissures, crevices around buildings and bat boxes. Winter roosts recorded in rock crevices, walls, caves, trees and log piles. May make seasonal migrations of up to 1,600 km (1,000 miles).
Breeding Maternity colonies of fifty to 200 move frequently. Males defend autumn mating roosts.
Food Assumed to eat small to medium-sized insects.
Conservation Threatened.
Similar species Common Pipistrelle *P. pipistrellus.*

Kuhl's Pipistrelle
Pipistrellus kuhlii

Size head & body 40–47 mm (1.5–1.75 ins);
    forearm 31–36 mm (1.25–1.5 ins)
Weight 5–10 g (0.25–0.5 oz)

Identification Typical small pipistrelle with upper fur variable
from medium or yellow brown to cinnamon-brown, often with
pale tips. Outer upper incisor much smaller than the inner one,
which is simple (in common and Nathusius's, it is bicuspid).
Range In Europe it occurs in south and south-west, over much
of France, Iberia, Switzerland, Italy, Austria and western
former Yugoslavia to Greece. On main Mediterranean islands,
but not Crete or Cyprus.
Habitat Rocky areas and human settlements to about 1000 m
(3,250 ft).
Behaviour Summer maternity colonies of twenty to a hundred
females have been found in crevices around buildings and in
cliffs, trees and bat boxes. Winter roosts have been seen in rock
crevices and cellars.
Breeding One of the few species where the female commonly
bears two young.
Food Emerges early and presumed to take quite small flying
insects from lower tree canopy, among houses, low over water
and around street lights.
Conservation Threatened.
Similar species Common Pipistrelle *P. pipistrellus* and
Nathusius's Pipistrelle *P. nathusii* (see pages 46, 47).

Savi's Pipistrelle
Pipistrellus savii

Size head & body 40–54 mm (1.5–2.25 ins);
     forearm 31–40 mm (1.25–1.5 ins)
Weight 5–10 g (0.25–0.5 oz)

Identification Ears more broadly rounded than in other
pipistrelles. Tragus is short, broadened with tip curved inwards
and serrated at the base of the outer edge. Fur is dense and
long, dark brown and often with golden tips. Ventral fur pale
in sharp contrast. Tail extending beyond margin of tail
membrane.

Range In Europe it is principally a Mediterranean species,
found in Iberia (except south-west), south-eastern France,
Switzerland, Austria, Italy, the Balkans, major Mediterranean
islands.
Habitat Woodland and pasture in valleys and mountains to
2,500 m (8,100 ft), in rocky areas especially near coasts and
around human habitation.
Behaviour Summer maternity colonies of twenty to seventy in
crevices around buildings, cliffs and trees. Winter roosts
recorded in cliff crevices and caves.
Breeding Females regularly bear two young.
Food Emerges early and hunts higher (at or above tree
canopy) and in more open situations than other pipistrelles.
Diet is presumed to be small flying insects.
Conservation Threatened.
Similar species Quite distinct from other pipistrelle species
(and sometimes put in a separate genus, *Hypsugo*). Similar to
Northern Bat *E. nilssonii* (see page 53).

Leisler's Bat
Nyctalus leisleri

Size head & body 48–68 mm (2–2.75 ins);
forearm 38–47 mm (1.5–2 ins)
Weight 11–20 g (0.5–0.75 oz)

Identification Short ears and mushroom-shaped tragus as in noctule bat, but fur not so short and sleek. The fur is darker at the base than at the tip. Wings are long and narrow and distinctly furred along the sides under the body and along the forelimbs, for which it can be called the Hairy-armed Bat.
Range Widespread but patchy distribution in Europe, including British Isles, central and southern Europe, Corsica, Madeira and Azores. Azores populations usually regarded as separate species, *N. azoreum.*

Habitat Open woodland to 2,000 m (6,500 ft), more often in urban areas than the noctule.
Behaviour Summer maternity roosts of twenty to fifty, or up to 500, usually in tree-holes, but may also be in buildings and bat boxes. Winter roosts in tree holes and the crevices of building and rock faces. Unpredictable migrant.
Breeding Males hold autumn territory to attract harem. Twin births quite common.
Food Emerges early and flies high at 3–15 m (10–45 ft) and fast, swooping to catch insects. Often feeds around street lights.
Conservation Protected throughout Europe.
Similar species Noctule Bat *N. noctula*

Noctule Bat
Nyctalus noctula

Size head & body 60–82 mm (2.25–3.25 ins);
    forearm 47–58 mm (2–2.25 ins)
Weight 19–40 g (0.75-1.5 oz)

Identification Sleek, short fur with hairs of uniform colour
throughout their length. Upper fur usually bright golden-
brown, ventral fur is slightly paler. Broad lobe at outer margin
of base of ear extends to corner of mouth. Tragus much
broadened at tip to mushroom shape. Penis long and narrow.
Range Widespread in Europe, from 60°N to the Balkans and
central Mediterranean, but scarce in Iberia and southern
France. Also on Corsica, Sardinia and Sicily. Throughout
Britain, but scarce in Scotland and absent from Ireland.
Habitat Deciduous woodland and park land near wetlands up
to 2,000 m (6,500 ft).
Behaviour Summer roosts are usually in tree-holes, but also in
bat boxes and buildings. Hibernates, sometimes in large
clusters, in tree-holes, rock crevices and buildings. Migrates up
to 1,500 km (1,000 miles).
Breeding Males display at autumn territories. Twins frequent
in north-east.
Food One of first bats to emerge and can be seen feeding with
swifts, swallows and martins high in the sky. Takes large
beetles, flies, crickets and large moths.
Conservation Becoming
rare in some areas.
Similar species
Other *Nyctalus* species.

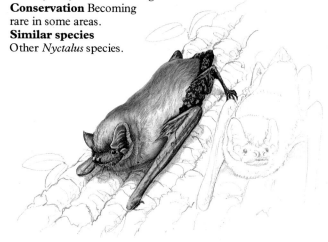

Greater Noctule Bat
Nyctalus lasiopterus

Size head & body 84–104 mm (3.25–4 ins);
forearm 62–70 mm (2.5–2.75 ins)
Weight 41–76 g (1.5–3 oz)

Identification The largest European bat. Similar to the
noctule with fur of uniform colour, but longer and deep
reddish brown. Flight membrane is dark and well furred with
rusty coloured hairs on underside along the body. Post-calcarial
lobe present (as in other *Nyctalus* species).
Range Scarce and sporadic from France, Germany, Poland
and the European CIS southwards to the Middle East and
North Africa. Mostly recorded from south-eastern and south-
western Europe.

Habitat Woodland to about 2,000 m (6,500 ft).
Behaviour Roosts have been found all year round in tree-
holes and also in buildings in summer. Migrates but little is
known of this aspect of behaviour.
Breeding Known nursery roosts number about ten, and
females have one or two young.
Food Feeds high, catching and eating large insects in flight.
Conservation Unknown.
Similar species Noctule Bat *N. noctula* (see page 51).

Northern Bat
Eptesicus nilssonii

Size head & body 54–64 mm (2.25–2.5 ins);
      forearm 37–44 mm (1.5–1.75 ins)
Weight 8–18 g (0.25–0.75 oz)

Identification Similar to larger serotine. The upper fur is long and shaggy, dark brown with glossy golden tips, clearly demarcated on the neck from the yellow ventral fur. Upper surface of tail membrane is lightly furred for about half its length. Unlike *Nyctalus* species, the penis is short and broad, and the thumb is long and slender. The outer upper incisor is about two-thirds the length of the inner. Tragus short and blunt, broadened near base. Tail extended beyond margin of tail membrane.
Range From 70°N in Scandinavia south to Denmark, Germany, Hungary and Romania. May be resident in Switzerland, but rare vagrant in Italy, France and Britain.
Habitat Woodland to 2,000 m (6,500 ft) and open areas with water, usually near habitation.
Behaviour The winter roosts are generally in cold and dry stores and cellars, caves and tunnels. Not a marked migrant but some long-range movements occur, perhaps in response to very cold weather.
Breeding Maternity colonies are in crevices in buildings or tree-holes, rock fissures and log piles. May contain up to one hundred females, but they move frequently.
Food Emerges early to feed at about 10 m (32 ft) or less. Food includes small flies, moths, beetles and caddisflies.
Similar species Serotine Bat *E. serotinus*, Savi's Pipistrelle *Pipistrellus savii* (see pages 54, 49).

Serotine Bat
Eptesicus serotinus

Size head & body 60–82 mm (2.5–3.25 ins);
     forearm 47–57 mm (2–2.25 ins)
Weight 14–35 g (0.5–1.25 oz)

Identification Large and robust with long shaggy fur. Dorsal fur is rich chocolate-brown with chestnut tips and poorly demarcated from paler ventral fur. Penis is short and bulbous. Curved tragus almost parallel-sided and blunt-tipped. Tail extended beyond tail membrane. Outer incisor is less than half the height of the inner.

Range Throughout Europe, south from Denmark and Sweden to some Mediterranean islands. Widespread in the south of Britain, particularly south of the River Thames. Absent from Ireland.

Habitat Pasture, meadow, park land, woodland edges and gardens below 1,000 m (3,250 ft).

Behaviour Summer roosts are almost always in buildings. Occasionally tree-holes, and in the south it is frequent in caves. Probably winters in buildings, but small numbers also found in caves, tunnels, log piles and scree. More or less sedentary but some long-range movements recorded.

Breeding Maternity colonies usually comprise fifteen to twenty bats, but can be larger. One young per female.

Food Preferentially large beetles and moths but also takes a range of small insects, particularly flies.

Conservation
May be spreading in north-western Europe.

Similar species
The very similar North American BIG BROWN BAT *E. fuscus* has been recorded in Europe after ship-assisted passage.

Parti-coloured Bat
Vespertilio murinus

Size head & body 48–64 mm (2–2.5 ins);
forearm 36–44 mm (1.5–1.75 ins)
Weight 12-20g

Identification Dorsal fur is long and very dark with silvery
tips, and in strong contrast to creamy-white ventral fur. The
female is unique among European bats in having two pairs of
nipples. Tragus short, broadened towards blunt tip. The penis
is not markedly bulbous.
Range From about 60°N in Finland and Scandinavia south to
Denmark in the west and further south in east. A few records
from Britain, the Netherlands, eastern France, north-east Italy.

Habitat Eroded hillsides and steppes to 2,000 m (6,500 ft),
but also agricultural land and parks.
Behaviour Winters in caves and tunnels, occasionally tree-
holes, but generally in small numbers. A migrant, moving up
to 900 km (500 miles) south-west and west in autumn.
Breeding Summer maternity colonies of thirty to fifty are
usually in crevices around buildings, in rock faces and
sometimes in trees. Most females give birth to twins and
occasionally triplets. Males territorial in autumn and will
occupy city tower blocks, making audible song flights that are
unique among European bats.
Food Usually emerges late and varies feeding behaviour in
order to concentrate on larger beetles and moths.

Western Barbastelle
Barbastella barbastellus

Size head & body 45–58 mm (1.75–2.25 ins);
forearm 39–49 mm (1.5–2 ins)
Weight 8–14 g (0.25–0.5 oz)

Identification Unmistakable, with long sleek, black-brown upper fur with frosted pale tips and only slightly paler below. The muzzle is very short and pug-like, with the nostrils opening more or less upwards. The ears are joined at the base and the outer edge usually has a small but distinct lobe about halfway up.

Range Most of Europe from the Mediterranean to about 60°N in Scandinavia, but absent from southern Spain and much of the Balkans. Also on Corsica, Sardinia and Sicily and perhaps other Mediterranean islands. Widespread but erratic in England and Wales.
Habitat Wooded foothills and mountains to about 2,000 m (6,500 ft), particularly in riparian woodland edges, avenues and park land.
Behaviour Hibernates in caves, tunnels and tree-holes usually in very cold sites. It is often solitary in cracks or on walls, but may form clusters of up to 500.
Breeding Summer maternity colonies of ten to twenty (sometimes more than a hundred) in roof spaces and crevices in buildings, tree-holes, bat boxes and caves.
Food Emerges early and hunts up to tree-top level over water or around edges of woodland or buildings. Takes relatively small insects, including moths, flies and beetles.
Conservation Regarded as one of the most endangered bat species in Europe.

Brown Long-eared Bat
Plecotus auritus

Size head & body 40–53 mm (1.5–2 ins);
  forearm 34–42 mm (1.25–1.75 ins)
Weight 6–15 g (0.25–0.5 oz)

Identification The extremely long ears are joined at the base and may be folded or curled back when at rest. The tragus is narrower than in the grey long-eared bat, the outer margin near the apex is straight. Ears and tragus rather translucent. The long, fluffy upper fur is brown-grey at the base tipped light brownish grey. The muzzle is long and bare with nostrils that open upwards. The thumb is long.
Range Most of Europe from about 64°N to northern Iberia, central Italy and former Yugoslavia. Widespread in Britain and Ireland.
Habitat Open woodland, park land and gardens.
Behaviour In winter some are found in buildings, trees, caves and tunnels, mostly solitarily and in cold sites.
Breeding Summer maternity colonies are found in tree-holes, attics and walls, bird boxes and bat boxes. Such roosts usually also contain males and colonies are usually rather small.
Food Emerge late and usually feed low, hovering among vegetation and taking quite large moths, caterpillars, beetles, spiders, caddisflies and true flies, which it takes to a regular feeding roost.
Conservation Relatively common species, but vulnerable.
Similar species Grey Long-eared Bat *P. austriacus* (see page 58).

Grey Long-eared Bat
Plecotus austriacus

Size head & body 41–58 mm (1.5–2.25 ins);
forearm 37–45 mm (1.5–1.75 ins)
Weight 7–14 g (0.25–0.5 oz)

Identification Slightly larger than the brown long-eared bat.
The tragus has a minimum width of 5.5 mm (0.22 ins), the
outer margin is distinctly emarginated. The thumb is short.
The upper fur is dark grey at the base and paler grey,
somewhat brown-tinged, towards the tip. The young of both
species of long-eared bats are much greyer than the adults.
Range The two species were only recently separated so their
distributions are confused in some areas. This species appears
to be more common in central and southern Europe, but
reaches north to about 53°N and south to the Mediterranean
and Balkans. It occurs rarely on the coast of Britain from
Sussex to Devon.
Habitat Open deciduous woodland and cultivated areas to
1,000 m (3,250 ft), where it prefers warmer valleys.
Behaviour Hibernation recorded in cold areas of caves,
tunnels, buildings and tree-holes.
Breeding Maternity colonies comprise ten to fifty bats, and
the two long-eared bat species have been found together.
Food Emerges late and flies low, catching moths, flies, beetles
and other insects. Larger prey is taken to a feeding roost.
Similar species Brown Long-eared Bat *P. auritus* (see page
57). Bechstein's Bat *Myotis bechsteinii* (see page 40).has long,
but clearly separated ears.

Schreiber's Bent-winged Bat
Miniopterus schreibersii

Size head & body 50–61 mm (2–2.5 ins);
forearm 43–48 mm (1.75–2 ins)
Weight 9–16 g (0.25–0.5 oz)

Identification The fur is short, silky and dense and grey-brown. The ventral fur is paler, sometimes with a pale or cinnamon-brown patch on the throat and forehead. Blunt muzzle with high domed forehead. Ears short and broadly rounded. The tragus is short and kidney-shaped and yellowish white to pale grey. The wings are very long and narrow. Second phalanx of third digit is about three times the length of the first. At rest the third and fourth digits are bent backwards at the joint between the first and second phalanges.

Range Mediterranean region north to central France, Switzerland, Austria, south-eastern Slovakia and Romania.
Habitat Open limestone hilly areas to 1,000 m (3,250 ft), scrubby woodland and steppe.
Behaviour Winters in fairly warm sites in caves, often in large clusters, and moves frequently, often over long distances.
Breeding Maternity roosts are nearly always in caves, occasionally in buildings, and may contain more than 1,000 individuals.
Food Emerges early and flies fast at 10–20 m (32–65 ft), taking moths, small flies and beetles.
Conservation Vulnerable cave bat.

European Free-tailed Bat
Tadarida teniotis
Chiroptera, Molossidae

Size head & body 81–92 mm (3.25–3.5 ins);
    forearm 57–64 mm (2.25–2.5 ins)
Weight 25–50 g (1–2 oz)

Identification Very large and robust, and the only European
member of a mainly tropical family. The ears are long and
broad and point forwards; the ear bases are connected and
there is a broad, distinctly furred flange on the outer margin
and a wrinkled flap at the base. The fur is short and velvety,
and the tail membrane reaches to only about half to two-thirds
the length of the long thick tail. Has a strong musky odour.
Wings long and narrow, feet strong and bristly.
Range Mediterranean region, including Iberia, south-eastern
France, Switzerland, Italy, the Balkans and most major
Mediterranean islands.
Habitat Rocky places to 2,000 m (6,500 ft); often seen in towns.
Behaviour The species probably does not hibernate, and it
may be a partial migrant.
Breeding Breeds in crevices in cliffs and caves and also in
buildings, bridges and water towers, usually in colonies of
fewer than fifty individuals.
Food Flies high and fast in open areas, sometimes over water.
Conservation Poorly known species.

Barbary Ape
Macaca sylvanus
Primates; Cercopithecidae

Size head & body 550–750 mm (22–30 ins)
Weight 10–15 kg (11–22 lb)

Identification The only European primate: a thickset animal with thick, shaggy fur and no visible tail.
Range In Europe it is found only on Gibraltar, where it is believed to have been introduced from Morocco in about 1740.
Habitat Scrubby rocky hillsides in Gibraltar, but elsewhere hills with coniferous and oak woodland.
Behaviour Diurnal and on Gibraltar some are habituated to human presence.
Breeding Mating is not seasonal, but most young are born in summer and nursed for about a year.
Food Mainly leaves, shoots, bulbs, but also seeds, fruit and some insects, scorpions and other small invertebrates.
Conservation Supplementary feeding and veterinary care are given to maintain the two colonies on Gibraltar. Endangered in its native North Africa.
Similar species None.

Grey Wolf
Canis lupus
Carnivora; Canidae

Size head and body 800–1400 mm (32–55 ins);
tail 300–500 mm (12–20 ins)
Weight 20–80 kg (44–176 lb)

Identification Like a large Alsatian dog, but ears shorter and
less pointed, head broader, exaggerated by a ruff of long hair
behind the cheeks. Head held low on a short thick neck and the
chest is shallow. Tail large, bushy and drooping. Characteristic
mournful howl especially during the mating season.
Range In Europe now only exists in isolated populations
(some very small) in Iberia, Italy, Balkans north to the Baltic
states, Finland and into Scandinavia.

Habitat Extensive, mainly montane, forests and tundra.
Behaviour Principally nocturnal and partially social, hunting
in packs of up to twenty animals in northern areas, particularly
in winter.
Breeding Adults pair for life, mating from January to March,
and litters of five to six young are born in a den in a cave,
under rocks or roots, or in a burrow.
Food Reindeer, elk, hares, rodents, carrion and birds,
occasionally reptiles and amphibians, insects, roots and tubers.
Conservation Highly endangered and protected in most of
range.
Similar species The wolf might be confused with a large dog.
The Northern Jackal *C. aureus* is smaller, redder and with a
relatively shorter tail.

Northern Jackal
Canis aureus

Size head & body 600–1050 mm (24–41 ins);
tail 200–300 mm (8–12 ins)
Weight 10–15 kg (22–33 lb)

Identification Smaller than the wolf, and more slender and agile-looking. It has larger ears and a relatively shorter tail. The fur is generally more reddish. Makes high-pitched plaintive howls at dusk.
Range Greece, former Yugoslavia, Bulgaria and Hungary. Via the eastern Mediterranean to Africa and south-east Asia.
Habitat Open country with cover, including grassland, cultivated land and marshes; occasionally in thicker woodland, generally at a lower altitude than the wolf.
Behaviour Less social than the wolf, perhaps more like the fox. Generally nocturnal and territorial.
Breeding Pairs stay together for many years. They mate in January or February, and the litter of four to five young is born in April in a burrow in dense cover.
Food Small mammals, birds and their eggs, molluscs, fish and carrion. Occasional domestic sheep or goats and can be serious raiders of poultry. Some fruit is eaten.
Similar species The Wolf *C. lupus* is similar but larger and greyer, and the Red Fox *Vulpes vulpes* (see page 65) is redder with a longer tail.

Arctic Fox
Alopex lagopus

Size head & body 500–700 mm (20–27.5 ins);
   tail 280–330 mm (11–13 ins)
Weight 4.5–8 kg (10–17.5 lb)

Identification Smaller than red fox with shorter muzzle and short rounded ears. Tail of uniform colour. Greyish brown or greyish yellow above and dirty white below in summer; white in winter. Some ('blue') foxes are smoky grey all over throughout the year.

Range Mountains of Scandinavia and Jan Mayen Island, Bear Island and Spitzbergen. Circumpolar.

Habitat Arctic tundra, sea ice. Moves south to open forest and ice-free coasts in winter where it overlaps with the red fox.

Behaviour More social and much more nomadic than the red fox. Makes its den in rock fissures or in quite complex burrow systems.

Breeding Mating usually takes place in April with five to eight young born in late spring. There is often time for a second litter in July or August.

Food Mainly voles and lemmings, but in summer also nesting birds and their eggs. In winter, carrion, molluscs, shellfish and other food from the seashore.

Similar species The Red Fox *Vulpes vulpes* is redder and usually more distinctly marked with a white tip to the tail, and pointed ears.

Red Fox
Vulpes vulpes

Size head & body 550–900 mm (22–36 ins);
tail 220–500 mm (9–20 ins)
Weight 3.5-10.0 kg (8–22 lb)

Identification Slender muzzle with black mark running from eye and white on nose and throat. Erect, pointed black-backed ears. Bushy tail often tipped white. Front of lower parts of legs black. Very characteristic lingering smell and a high-pitched, hacking, attenuated bark, especially in the rut.
Range Throughout mainland Britain and Ireland, but absent from many major Scottish islands, Isles of Scilly and Channel islands. From northern Scandinavia south to much of coastal North Africa (including many Mediterranean islands) and the Arabian Peninsula.

Habitat Woodland with cover as well as extensive open areas such as uplands (to the snow line) and dunes; may avoid desert and steppe. Spreading into urban environments.
Behaviour More or less solitary, but family groups share territory. Mainly crepuscular and nocturnal. Individuals often lay up in thick cover, but dens ('earths') are used particularly in the breeding season.
Breeding Four to five cubs are born in March or April. The nest has no bedding, and food remains and other 'play' items are often found around an earth with cubs.
Food Mainly small lagomorphs and rodents, but also birds and their eggs, beetles and other invertebrates, especially earthworms, and fruit. May scavenge, for example on sheep and deer. Surplus food is sometimes cached.
Similar species Arctic Fox *Alopex lagopus*.

Raccoon Dog
Nyctereutes procyanoides

Size head & body 550–750 mm (22–30 ins);
tail 150–250 mm (6–10 ins)
Weight 5–10 kg (11–22 lb)

Identification About the size of a red fox, but more heavily built with long shaggy fur, a short muzzle and short legs and ears. A tuft of long fur behind each eye and a large patch of black on the sides of the face give it a masked appearance.
Range Widely established from introductions and escapes in Finland, Sweden, Denmark and France, through Germany, Switzerland, Poland, the Czech Republic, Slovakia and Hungary to Romania. Native to warmer parts of eastern Asia.
Habitat Broad-leaved forest, coniferous woodland and scrub, especially near wetlands.
Behaviour More or less solitary and semi-nomadic. Nocturnal and inactive for quite long periods in the winter.
Breeding Mating takes place in April or earlier, and six to eight young are born in June in a burrow.
Food Small vertebrates, including rodents, frogs, birds' eggs and fish, invertebrates including earthworms, vegetable matter such as fruit, nuts and bulbs, and some carrion.
Similar species The Common Raccoon *Procyon lotor* has a slightly different, more contrasting facial pattern and a bushy ringed tail.

Common Raccoon
Procyon lotor
Carnivora; Procyonidae

Size head & body 500–700 mm (20–28 ins);
tail 200–600 mm (8–24 ins)
Weight 3–10 kg (6.5–22 lb)

Identification About the size of a large cat with a long bushy
tail which is banded black and white. Black mask through eyes
and conspicuous cheek tufts. The stout body is clothed in quite
long dirty grey-brown fur and the legs are short.
Range Native to North America, it escaped from captivity and
established wild populations in Germany (Eifel) and spread
from there to adjacent France, Netherlands and Luxembourg;
and is still spreading. It is also feral in parts of Asiatic CIS and
sometimes within Britain.

Habitat Woodland, especially by rivers and streams.
Behaviour Generally in family groups and is principally
nocturnal. In the winter, activity is much reduced although it
does not hibernate. Good swimmer and climber, often denning
above ground.
Breeding Mating occurs from January to March, and three to
seven young are born in March or April.
Food Molluscs, insects, crayfish, fish, small mammals
(especially rodents), eggs and young of ground-nesting birds,
frogs and earthworms. It also feeds on fruit and nuts (especially
acorns) and grain.
Similar species The Raccoon Dog *Nyctereutes procyanoides*
has a different facial pattern and an unbanded tail.

Brown Bear
Ursos arctos
Carnivora; Ursidae

Size head & body 1.5–2.5 m (5–8 ft);
    tail 60–140 mm (2.5–5.5 ins)
Weight 100–400 kg (220–880 lb)

Identification Heavily built with thick legs and neck and no obvious tail. The shaggy fur is very dark brown to pale creamy fawn, usually a dark yellowish brown.
Range Main European populations now restricted to the Balkans, with four other small southern groups (Pyrenees, Italian Alps, Cantabria and Abruzzi National Park).

There are also small populations in Scandinavia and in the Tatra and Carpathian Mountains.
Habitat Mainly a forest animal, but visits open tundra in the north or to above the tree line on mountains.
Behaviour Generally solitary, territorial and mainly nocturnal. Swims well, but rarely climbs (except when young). Spends extended periods of winter inactive in a den excavated under a rock or tree, or in a cave.
Breeding About two young born in January or February in the winter den. The young stay with the mother through their first winter and the female breeds in alternate years.
Food Omnivorous: green plant material, roots, tubers, bulbs, fruit and nuts, fungi and grain. Animal food includes small items: ants and other insects, honey, frogs, small mammals, birds' eggs and fish; occasionally larger mammals or carrion.
Conservation Generally highly protected.
Similar species Young are similar to the Wolverine *Gulo gulo* (see page 79), which has an obvious tail.

Polar Bear
Thalarctos maritimus

Size head & body 1.5–2.8 m (5–9 ft);
    tail 80–100 mm (3–4 ins)
Weight 400–600 kg (880–1320 lb)

Identification Very large with long white or yellowish white
fur.
Range Circumpolar, where it occurs on sea-ice and coasts of
the Arctic Sea. In European areas it only occurs as far south as
Spitzbergen and Novaya Zemblya, but wanders extensively on
ice and has been recorded on the northern coast of Norway.
Habitat Almost entirely marine, on the coasts and sea-ice as
far north as there is open water, and seldom more than 1–2 km
(0.5–1.25 miles) inland.
Behaviour Solitary and very nomadic. Very agile on the ice,
but usually walks slowly, head down and waggling from side to
side. It can gallop for short distances, swim very well and can
dive for up to two minutes.
Breeding Mating occurs in July, and one to two young are
born in February in a short burrow in the snow. Infants emerge
in March and remain with the female for about one year.
Food Seals and fish are most important. Occasionally rodents,
reindeer, foxes and birds are taken. Sometimes eats carrion and
occasionally will cache food. Also eats small quantities of algae
and moss.

Stoat
Mustela erminea
Carnivora; Mustelidae

Size head & body 200–300 mm (8–12 ins);
 tail 60–140 mm (2.25–5.5 ins)
Weight 100–445 g (4–16 oz)

Identification The fur is rich russet to ginger brown above, usually clearly demarcated from the creamy white fur of the underside, which may be reduced to a narrow ventral stripe in the Irish stoat. In the north, it moults to a white fur in winter retaining black tail-tip.
Range Throughout Europe including mainland British Isles, but absent from some of the larger Scottish islands and the Mediterranean peninsulas.

Habitat Anywhere with cover and prey, using hedgerows, stone walls, ditch and road banks to traverse open spaces. Generally avoids mature woodland.
Behaviour Runs with an arched-back bounding gait, sometimes standing on its hind legs to investigate surroundings. Usually silent, but can produce a range of harsh or high-pitched trills. Generally solitary and territorial.
Breeding Mating in May or June, but implantation of the embryo is delayed, and the birth of five to ten young occurs between April and May.
Food In Britain, the rabbit is the major prey, elsewhere smaller mammals, especially voles, are more important. Also takes birds, occasionally worms or fruit. Often caches large numbers of surplus prey.
Similar species The black-tipped tail is relatively longer than in the Weasel *M. nivalis*.

Weasel
Mustela nivalis

Size head & body 145–230 mm (5.75–9 ins);
   tail 30–75 mm (1.25–3 ins)
Weight 35–200 g (1.25–7 oz)

Identification Like the stoat, but much smaller with a
relatively shorter tail without a black tip. The male is nearly
twice the size of the female. The fur is a dull russet to ginger
brown above, white or cream below. Sometimes with brown
spots and blotches on belly. The coat turns white in winter in
northern and eastern Eurasia, but not as far south as the stoat
and rarely in Britain.
Range Throughout Europe including mainland Britain, but
absent from Ireland, the Isle of Man and most of the Scottish
islands.
Habitat Wider range of habitats, although it is less common
on high mountains and in woodland with little ground cover.
Behaviour Generally solitary and territorial. Active day and
night for brief periods separated by longer rest periods.
Breeding Mates between March and August and one or two
litters of four to eight young are born. Population fluctuates
due to changes in rodent populations.
Food Small rodents (particularly voles), sometimes birds or
their eggs, rabbits (particularly young ones) and rats.
Similar species Smaller than the Stoat *M. erminea* and
without a black tip to the tail.

European Mink
Mustela lutreola

Size head & body: 320–450 mm (12–18 ins);
    tail 130–220 mm (5–8.75 ins)
Weight 450–1500 g (1–3 lb)

Identification Typical mustelid appearance, but with a rather bushy tail about half the length of the body. The fur is glossy chocolate brown, almost black, with white on the muzzle, chin and chest.
Range Now only in parts of Spain, western France, Romania, possibly Finland and the CIS.

Habitat Marshes and well-vegetated banks of rivers and lakes, especially those associated with woodland.
Behaviour Semi-aquatic, solitary, nocturnal, territorial. Shy and occasionally makes a piping alarm note. Dens near water in dense reed, rock clefts, holes in banks, tree roots. Occasionally excavates its own burrow.
Breeding Most mating is in February and March, and four to five young are born in April or June.
Food Water vole, musk rat, rats, waterside birds, amphibians and fish, with occasional invertebrates such as crayfish or molluscs.
Conservation Declining, probably due to deterioration and pollution of its habitat, competition with the stronger American mink, and trapping efforts to control species such as coypu (see page 178), muskrat (see page 148) and American mink.
Similar species AMERICAN MINK *M. vison* is widely introduced (including Britain). The white of the muzzle is usually confined to the lower jaw, but the two species can be very difficult to separate.

Ferret
Mustela furo

Size head & body 225–450 mm (9–18 ins);
tail 100–160 mm (4–6.5 ins)
Weight 400–1500 g (0.75–3 lb)

Identification In general appearance similar to both the
polecat and the steppe polecat. Pelage is usually more or less
white or cream, including albino forms with pink eyes.
Sometimes darker with a polecat-like pattern.
Range Widely in Europe as an escapee, but rarely establishes
viable populations, especially where the polecat occurs. It has
established mainland feral populations from time to time and
other populations survive on islands around Britain, such as.
Anglesey, Mull, Lewis, Bute, Arran, Isle of Man, and the
Mediterranean, such as Sardinia and Sicily.
Habitat As an escapee, it can occur in almost any environment
from high-density urban habitats to the open moorland habitat
of many island populations.
Behaviour Being of domestic origin, the ferret is often
relatively tame and even inquisitive.
Breeding Similar to polecat and will interbreed, but the young
are usually infertile.
Food Similar to polecat.
Conservation May have deleterious effects on native polecats.
Similar species The pale forms are distinct, but some of the
darker forms are indistinguishable in the field from the Western
Polecat *M. putorius* (see page 74).

Western Polecat
Mustela putorius

Size head & body 225–460 mm (9–18 ins);
tail 100–165 mm (4–6.5 ins)
Weight 400–1800 g (0.75–4 lb)

Identification The fur appears mainly dark, almost iridescent
black, but the underfur is actually very pale. The ears have a
white margin, there are white cheek patches which may almost
meet over the top of the head and the muzzle is pale.
Range From southern Sweden and Finland through Europe
(except Greece, coastal former Yugoslavia and Bulgaria) to
about 70°E. In Britain, only in Wales, but may be spreading.

Habitat Broad-leaved or mixed woodland including forest
plantations, but also in farmland, marshes, overgrown
embankments, open moorland, cliff and dune areas, and even
towns and cities.
Behaviour Shy, usually solitary and generally crepuscular or
nocturnal species. Dens vary from casual resting places on the
ground to excavated lairs with compartments, which,
particularly in winter, are often under or around buildings.
Breeding Mating usually takes place in March or April, and
five to ten young are cared for by the female alone.
Food Rabbits and hares, small rodents, birds and fish, eggs of
birds and some reptiles and amphibians.
Conservation Severe persecution has followed predation of
game birds and poultry.
Similar species Some dark Ferrets *M. furo* (see page 73) are
indistinguishable in the field.

Steppe Polecat
Mustela eversmanni

Size head & body 260–770 mm (10–30 ins);
tail 80–170 mm (3–6.5 ins)
Weight 330–1500 g (0.75–3 lb)

Identification Upper fur is yellowish brown; underside, fore
and hind limbs dark. Muzzle and ears whitish and there are
yellowish brown patches over the eyes. The tail is light at the
base, but black-brown on the terminal half.
Range Steppes of eastern Europe in Austria, Hungary and
Czechoslovakia eastwards. Occasional records from Poland (in
the Lublin Upland), eastern Germany and Romania.
Habitat Open country, avoiding forest and built-up areas.
Behaviour Digs its own short burrows or occupies those of
other animals. The entrance is often marked by excavated
earth, excrement and food remains. Most active at dawn and
dusk and may remain in the burrow for several days in hard
weather.
Breeding Mating occurs in February and March and eight to
eleven young are born in late April.
Food Mainly sousliks, hamsters and small rodents, but also
other mammals up the size of hare, birds and their eggs,
reptiles, amphibians, fish and insects. Surplus food may be
cached.
Similar species Similar to the Western Polecat *M. putorius,*
but paler in colour, though variable. The dark legs and chest
differentiate it from the Pine Marten *Martes martes* or Beech
Marten *Martes foina* (see pages 77, 78).

Marbled Polecat
Vormela peregusna

Size head & body 300–380 mm (12–15 ins);
tail 150–200 mm (6–8 ins)
Weight 370–700 g (13–25 oz)

Identification The facial and body patterns makes it very distinct from the western polecat and steppe polecat. Mouth white, white stripe from above eye to sides of neck, more prominent ears white. Back with red-brown or black-brown background boldly mottled with yellow or white.The underside is a uniform black brown. The bushy tail is yellowish or white-sided and with a black tip.
Range Parts of Romania, Bulgaria, former Yugoslavia and northern Greece.
Habitat Dry grassland, scrub and open woodland, sometimes in gardens and cultivation (such as maize fields, orchards and vineyards).
Behaviour Similar to the steppe polecat. It frequently sits up or stands on its hind legs, is able to climb well, and throws its tail upwards when excited.
Breeding Mating takes place in late spring, and four to eight young are born by the following March after a long-delayed pregnancy.
Food Voles and mice (especially gerbils) and other rodents up to the size of small hares, birds (particularly quail), lizards and insects such as mole crickets. Will hoard food.

Pine Marten
Martes martes

Size head & body 360–540 mm (14–21 ins);
   tail 170–270 mm (7–11 ins)
Weight 700–1950 g (1.5–4.5 lb)

Identification Longer legged than *Mustela* species. Head flatter with a longer more pointed muzzle. Rich, dark brown fur with cream or orange chest and throat patch, large, rounded pale-edged ears and long bushy tail.
Range Forested areas of Europe, including most major Mediterranean islands; absent Spain and Greece. Relict distribution in the British Isles (Scotland, Cumbria, Yorkshire, Wales and coastal Ireland).
Habitat Older mixed coniferous or deciduous forest; also pasture, scrub, moorland.
Behaviour Solitary, nocturnal, very agile and a good climber. Dens in rock falls, trees, squirrel or crow nests in trees and owl boxes. Sometimes found in outbuildings and lofts.
Breeding Mates in July and August, but implantation of the embryo is delayed, and one to five young appear in the following March or April.
Food Mainly small rodents (sometimes squirrels, rabbits and hares), birds (including their eggs), beetles, berries and fungi. Occasionally raids bees' nests for honey. Sometimes feeds from bird-tables.
Conservation Endangered in parts of range.
Similar species Many Mediterranean island populations sometimes distinguished as distinct species: *M. latinorum* (Sardinia and Corsica); *M. minorcensis* (Menorca); *M. arculus* (Crete); and *M.rhodius. (*Rhodes).
SABLE *M. zibellina* is darker with an ill-defined white throat and chest patch, and now only occurs naturally in the CIS.

Beech Marten
Martes foina

Size head & body 400–480 mm (16–19 ins);
tail 220–260 mm (8.5–10.5 ins)
Weight 1300–2300 g (3–5 lb)

Identification Like the pine marten, but white throat and chest patch often divided by a vertical dark stripe. It is heavier built with shorter legs and is not so agile. The ears are narrower and smaller.
Range Southern and central Europe, but occurs as far north as the English Channel and the Baltic coast. Isolated populations on Crete, Rhodes and Corfu; the Ibiza population is sometimes regarded as a separate species.
Habitat Deciduous woodland, open rocky hillsides up to 2,400 m (7,800 ft). It is more frequent around buildings than the pine marten and even enters towns.
Behaviour Nocturnal. A little more 'domestic' than the pine marten: its dens are more often in buildings, although it also uses rock falls, hollow trees and, rarely, digs its own burrow. Much less arboreal than the pine marten.
Breeding One litter of one to eight young born in the spring following long-delayed implantation period.
Food Mice and other rodents to the size of squirrels, shrews, birds, reptiles and amphibians, invertebrates and berries.
Similar species Pine Marten *M. martes* (see page 77), but has a more southern distribution.

Wolverine
Gulo gulo

Size head & body 700–900 mm (28–35 ins);
tail 125–300 mm (5–12 ins)
Weight 9–30 kg (20–66 lb)

Identification Shaggy, very dark brown fur; forehead and
cheeks a little paler and a broad, pale brown band runs along
the flanks and across the fairly short bushy tail. Might be
confused with a bear cub, but the pattern and the
inconspicuous rounded ears are distinctive.
Range Mountains of Norway and Sweden to about 58°N and
across Finland to the Baltic states. Also found across the CIS
and in North America.

Habitat Evergreen forests (or taiga), with associated birch
woodland and scrub. Often near marshes and roaming far
north into the tundra in summer.
Behaviour Mostly nocturnal, wandering widely with no
permanent burrow or den.
Breeding Mating seems to occur at almost anytime and
probably delayed implantation allows some synchronisation of
the birth of the young to between February or March, and
May. Two to three (or even five) young are born in a hollow
tree, among rocks or in sheltered snow drifts.
Food Small mammals, birds and their eggs, invertebrates such
as snails, and fruit, berries and fungi. It will feed on carrion and
caches surplus food. Occasionally it will scavenge in and
around buildings. Reported to take reindeer and elk in snow.

Badger
Meles meles

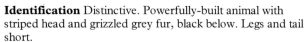

Size head & body 670–900 mm (26–35 ins);
   tail 110-200 mm (4–8 ins)
Weight 6.5–17 kg (14–37.5 lb)

Identification Distinctive. Powerfully-built animal with striped head and grizzled grey fur, black below. Legs and tail short.
Range In Britain and Ireland the badger is widespread except for some regions of higher altitude and some offshore islands. Found throughout mainland Europe except Norway and northern Sweden and Finland.
Habitat Very variable, but especially deciduous and mixed woodland and copses; also hedgerow, scrub and other places offering adequate cover and suitable well-drained soil.
Behaviour Nocturnal and social; digs complex and extensive tunnel systems (setts) with a number of entrances. There are well-marked trails around setts, sometimes discarded bedding near the entrance and the droppings are deposited in open shallow latrine pits.
Breeding Mating usually occurs in early spring, implantation of the embryo is delayed until December, and one to five young are born in February; they emerge from the sett in April.
Food Earthworms plus some small (mainly young) mammals, carrion (particularly in winter), other invertebrates, cereals, fruit, roots, tubers and corms. Occasionally birds, reptiles, amphibians, molluscs, fungi and green matter are eaten.
Conservation Widely protected, but often persecuted.

European Otter
Lutra lutra

Size head & body 530–1000 mm (20–39 ins);
tail 300–550 mm (12–22 ins)
Weight 5–17 kg (11–37.5 lb)

Identification Long slender body and long tail that tapers from a very thick base. The head is flat with small eyes and ears, the legs short with webbed feet. The sleek fur is mid-brown with a paler throat.
Range In the British Isles: throughout Ireland, most of Scotland, Wales (except the south) and patchy distribution in mainly coastal England. Throughout rest of Europe, but there has been a marked decline.
Habitat Lakes, rivers, streams, marshes and sheltered coasts.
Behaviour Mainly solitary and nocturnal, although coastal otters are often more active by day. The den (or holt) may be an underground tunnel or cavity under tree roots on a river bank, but otters also frequently use resting places on the surface (couches). A shrill whistle is well known as a contact call, but is rarely heard.
Breeding The litter of two to five young stay underground for about seven weeks.
Food Freshwater fish, crayfish, frogs. Sometimes birds (such as waterfowl, starlings and swallows roosting in reed beds) or mammals (including water vole and rabbit) are taken, as are carrion and insects. Marine fish and crabs.
Conservation Widely threatened, but recovering in some areas.
Similar species European Mink *Mustela lutreola* (see page 72) has longer fur and its tail is cylindrical and fluffy.

Small-spotted Genet
Genetta genetta
Carnivora; Viverridae

Size head & body 500–600 mm (20–23.5 ins);
    tail 400–500 mm (16–20 ins)
Weight 1–2.2 kg (2.5–4.5 lb)

Identification Sharply-pointed muzzle, spotted coat and a
very long, tapered, ringed tail. Slimmer and with shorter legs
than a cat.
Range Now restricted to southern and western France and
Iberia as well as Ibiza and Majorca. Generally regarded as a
separate species from that of the Middle East and sub-Saharan
Africa. Some argue that the European population is the result
of human introduction. The Ibiza population (also thought to
be an introduction) has been given separate subspecific status
as *G. g. isabelae*.
Habitat Woodland and rocky scrubs, often in moist woodland
with streams and boulders. Restricted to pine forests in Ibiza.
Behaviour An agile climber and leaps and swims well. More
or less solitary and territorial, and nocturnal. Dens in hollow
trees, rock cavities, under bushes or occasionally in trees.
Faeces are deposited in high conspicuous places, including the
roofs of buildings.
Breeding There may be two litters of two to three young a
year, one in April and one between August and September.
Food Birds, reptiles, rodents and many invertebrates, but fruits
and berries are also eaten. The Ibiza population feeds
particularly on reptiles and amphibians.

Egyptian Mongoose
Herpestes ichneumon
Carnivora; Herpestidae

Size head & body 500–600 mm (20–23.5 ins),
tail 350–450 mm (14–18 ins)
Weight 7–8 kg (15.5–17.5 lb)

Identification Similar to mink or polecats, but larger and with
a uniform coarse, grizzled dark grey-brown coat and a long
tapering black-tipped tail. Ears short and broad. The legs are
short and barely visible when the animal is moving.
Range An introduction from Africa and the Middle East to
southern Iberia, possibly by the Romans. It has also been

introduced to the island of Mljet and elsewhere in former
Yugoslavia.
Habitat Scrub, rocky and heath-covered hillsides, maquis and
woodland in river valleys.
Behaviour More or less solitary and terrestrial, and usually
digs its own short burrow.
Breeding Mating occurs in April, and births of two to four
young occur in July and August.
Food Lizards, snakes, small mammals to the size of a rabbit,
fish, birds and their eggs and insects.
Similar species The INDIAN GREY MONGOOSE *H. edwardsi*
was introduced from southern Asia to central Italy in the
1960s. It is slightly smaller (head and body about 450 mm
[17.5 in]) and has similar grizzled grey-brown fur, but a
relatively longer and paler-tipped tail. Another Indian species,
H. auropunctatus, has been introduced to Adriatic islands.

Wild Cat
Felis silvestris
Carnivora; Felidae

Size head & body 470–900 mm (18.5–36 ins);
tail 250–400 mm (10–16 ins)
Weight 5–10 kg (11–22 lb)

Identification Very like many domestic cat but larger and
heavier with a very square robust head and a relatively shorter
tail (about 40–45 per cent of the body length) which is very
bushy and blunt-tipped with three to five distinct black rings
and a black tip.
Range In Britain now confined to central and northern
mainland Scotland. Elsewhere in Europe it occurs in Iberia,
France, Italy and the Balkans to the Tatra and Carpathian
mountains. Populations on the Mediterranean islands of
Sardinia, Corsica and the Balearics are sometimes considered
as distinct species.

Habitat Although now mainly confined to montane forest in
the north it also lives on rocky mountain sides and moorland.
Behaviour Mainly terrestrial, generally solitary and territorial.
Breeding Mates in spring, and the litter of two to four is
usually born in May.
Food Small mammals to the size of hare. It may even take a
small roe deer kid or lamb. Birds, frogs, fish and insects are also
eaten. It will eat some grass or bracken.
Conservation Persecution, fragmentation of the woodlands
have led to decline.
Similar species The domestic cat may be a descendant of
Mediterranean forms of the wild cat.

Eurasian Lynx
Lynx lynx

Size head & body 800–1300 mm (31–51 ins);
   tail 110–250 mm (4–10 ins)
Weight 18–38 kg (40–84 lb)

Identification A large, long-legged cat with tufted ears and
cheeks and a short, black-tipped tail.
Range Now restricted to Scandinavia, Iberia, the Balkans and
doubtfully north to the Carpathians (including eastern Poland).
It may also still occur on Sardinia. Re-introductions in
Switzerland, France, Bavaria, former Yugoslavia, Austria,
western Germany, the Czech Republic and Slovakia.
Habitat Prefers large, coniferous, primeval forests on rocky
or mountainous ground, but also found in the low plains scrub
of the Coto Donana.
Behaviour Solitary and nocturnal. The den is a simple hollow
among rocks or in a tree, or sometimes just a scrape in dense
thicket; sometimes in caves or badger's sett.
Breeding Mating mostly in February or March, the female
gives birth to two or three kittens between the end of April and
June. Young stay with mother for about a year.
Food Hares, rabbits, rodents and ground birds. Young
ungulates, such as domestic animals and deer including
reindeer, are also taken.
Conservation Endangered and subject of intense conservation
programmes.
Similar species The Iberian form is heavily spotted and often
considered a separate species (*F. pardina*). The smaller, striped
Wild Cat *Felis silvestris* has a larger tail. The Grey Wolf *Canis
lupus* (see page 62) has a more pointed head and long tail.

Walrus

Odobenus rosmarus
Pinnipedia; Odobenidae

Size female to 2.5 m (8 ft), male to 4 m (13 ft)
Weight female to 800 kg (1,760 lb),
      male to 2,200 kg (4,850 lb)

Identification A familiar and unmistakable animal, but
rarely seen in Europe. Large flat moustachial pad with heavy
white whiskers. Tusks in both sexes. Able to swing hind
flippers forwards.
Range Arctic Ocean, following the ice southwards in winter.
It is a rare visitor to European waters, but there have been
about thirty records on the Norway coast in this century,
and a slightly larger number of records from Britain in the
last 175 years. There are also occasional records from
Germany, the Netherlands and Belgium.
Habitat Moving pack ice in shallower seas (less than 100 m
[300 ft] deep), but also rocky islands and occasionally
mainland beaches. Most European records are from sheltered
beaches of estuaries.
Behaviour Normally gregarious, but are only likely to be seen
in European waters as individuals.
Breeding Bulls attract groups of females by vocal display and
threat. Mating occurs between January and April, and young
are born more than a year later between April and June.
Food Molluscs collected from depths of up to 75 m (250 ft),
especially clams, rock borers and cockles. Smaller molluscs,
worms, echinoderms and polar cod are also taken.

Harbour Seal (Common Seal)
Phoca vitulina
Pinnipedia; Phocidae

Size 1.2–1.8 m (4–6 ft)
Weight 45–130 kg (100–290 lb)

Identification The harbour (or common) seal differs from the grey seal in its relatively shorter, rounder head with a distinct forehead and a snub nose. Nostrils V-shaped; spots quite small.
Range Circumpolar. In Europe from the British Isles and the Netherlands to northern Germany, the south-eastern Swedish coast and the entire coast of Norway. In Britain, the species is most common in East Anglia and via the north British coast (including Orkney and Shetland) to the Firth of Clyde and Ireland.

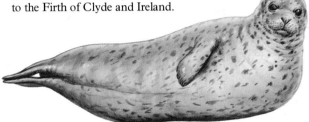

Habitat Shallow coastal waters, estuaries and tidal sandbanks, sometimes shingle beaches and rocky shores.
Behaviour Aggregate when ashore, but with almost no social organization. Rest with both head and tail raised. Fairly sedentary.
Breeding Mating promiscuous and usually takes place in the water, in autumn. Single pup born in June or July is ready to swim almost immediately.
Food Mainly fish; also squid, molluscs and crabs.
Conservation Populations estimated at 300,000–500,000 with about 5 per cent in Britain, but recent distemper virus severely set back the North Sea populations. Numbers are now recovering. There is conflict with fishermen because they take fish from nets.
Similar species Grey Seal *Halichoerus grypus* (see page 90).

Ringed Seal
Phoca hispida

Size 1.2–1.8 m (4–6 ft)
Weight 45–120 kg (100–260 lb)

Identification Very variable in colour, spotted with black, particularly on the back where the spots may be more or less contiguous. Many spots surrounded by ring-shaped lighter marks.
Range Circumpolar. In Europe it is found in the Baltic Sea and associated Gulfs of Bothnia and Finland (including into Lake Saimaa) and in northern Finland and Scandinavia.

Habitat Open water in fast ice, inshore waters of fiords and bays and into fresh water. Some stay under the ice in winter using breathing holes.
Behaviour Fairly solitary and non-migratory and seldom recorded outside its normal range; there are about ten records from the British Isles in the last 150 years, including Ireland, the Isle of Man and Norfolk. Stragglers have been recorded from France, Germany, the Netherlands, Portugal and Norway.
Breeding Most mating is from April to June, just after the birth of the young.
Food A wide variety of pelagic amphipods, euphausian shrimps, other crustaceans and small fish.
Conservation The most common seal of the Arctic seas (population estimated at between 3.5 and 7,000,000), but the lake populations (which some regard as a subspecies) and those of the Baltic Sea are threatened by pollution and development.

Harp Seal
Phoca groenlandica

Size 1.5–2 m (5–6.5 ft)
Weight 115–130 kg (250–290 lb)

Identification Variable in colour. Adult male light silvery grey over most of the body, with the front of the head to just behind the eye black and a black irregular horseshoe-shaped band ('harp') along the flanks and across the mantle. Face and 'harp' paler in female. Leaps through the water, like dolphins, when migrating.

Range Occurring in the North Atlantic and Arctic Oceans to about 120°E and 100°W, including northern coasts of Finland and Scandinavia. Stragglers occur in Norway (where there were large invasions in 1987 and 1988), Germany and the British Isles. About thirty-one records in British Isles since 1800, from Shetland islands, Scotland and around England and Ireland, including along the English Channel and some rivers, such as Devon's River Teign.

Habitat Coastal waters and rough hummocky ice with holes for access to sea.

Behaviour Migratory and forms large aggregations, although not particularly gregarious.

Breeding Mating promiscuous, and males appear on the ice in search of females soon after they have given birth. Single pups born in February or March.

Food Young animals take pelagic crustaceans (euphausian shrimps and amphipods) and some small fish. The more aggregated adults take more pelagic schooling fish.

Grey Seal
Halichoerus grypus

Size 1.7–3.2 m (5.5–10.5 ft)
Weight 105–310 kg (230–680 lb)

Identification Male up to half as large again as female and with high, convex, 'Roman' nose; female with almost straight profile to the top of the head. Nostrils more nearly parallel than in harbour seal.
Range North Atlantic. In Europe from north-western France via the British Isles, to the Faroes and Iceland, in the Baltic Sea and from about 60°N in Norway to the White Sea. The British Isles (mainly the north and west) holds 50–75 per cent of the world population.
Habitat Rocky coasts and caves, usually of islands, but sometimes on mainland beaches and also on fast or flowing ice.
Behaviour More terrestrial than the harbour seal. Breeding groups cluster densely, with old bulls maintaining a territory including a herd of females.
Breeding Mating occurs just after the end of lactation when the pup is deserted. Young are born from September to December in British Isles, from February to April in the Baltic.
Food Pelagic and mid-water fish; some bottom-living fish from as deep as 70 m (230 ft). Crustaceans, cephalopods and other molluscs also eaten.
Conservation Perceived competition for salmon with fishermen and damage to nets has led to persecution.

Bearded Seal
Erignathus barbatus

Size 2.2–2.5 m (7–8 ft)
Weight 235–300 kg (520–660 lb)

Identification A large species with a relatively small head; the female is only slightly smaller than the male. The striking feature is a well-developed moustachial pad bearing a large number of long, very white whiskers. Adults more or less uniformly coloured.
Range This is another circumpolar species, and in Europe stragglers occasionally appear on the northern Norway coast and as far south as Normandy. There are about ten records from the British Isles in the last twenty years (nearly all from Orkney and Shetland, but with early records as far south as Norfolk).

Habitat Shallow waters near coasts free of fast ice in winter, with gravel or rocky beaches, caves and close to ice-floes. Sometimes it travels long distances with ice.
Behaviour Not particularly social or gregarious, but forms small groups.
Breeding Breeds on ice floes, mating in the spring at the end of lactation. Pupping occurs from March to May.
Food Crabs and whelks, also shrimps, holothurians, clams, other molluscs, octopus and fish (including sculpin, flounder and polar cod) taken from depths of up to 130 m (425 ft). Some of the food is probably sucked in as with walrus.

Mediterranean Monk Seal
Monachus monachus

Size 2.3–2.8 m (7.5–9 ft)
Weight 300–400 kg (660–880 lb)

Identification Dark chocolate brown to black, generally
lighter underneath or with a variable whitish patch on the
belly. The nostrils form a broad V-shape more or less meeting
at the base.
Range Once widely distributed in Mediterranean, Black Sea
and off West Africa in Spanish Sahara, Madeira and possibly
the Azores. Now only found in the Mediterranean on islands of
the eastern Aegean and the Turkish coast.

Also recorded from Morocco, Algeria, Tunisia, the Balearic
islands, Sardinia and Sicily.
Habitat Traditionally sandy beaches, but in Europe is now
restricted to small islands with mainly rocky coastlines, where
it hauls out in caves and grottoes.
Behaviour It is now too late to learn about any social
organization in this species.
Breeding Mating seems to be promiscuous (and probably
occurs in the water), pups are usually born from September to
October (sometimes May and June).
Food Fish and octopus taken from waters to a depth of 30 m
(100ft).
Conservation Gravely endangered – probably fewer than 500
remain. Even the strongest populations (in Greece) are now
hardly viable due to disturbance, pollution and persecution.

Hooded Seal
Cystophora cristata

Size 2.2–2.7 m (8–9 ft)
Weight 200–400 kg (440–880 lb)

Identification The male is distinctly larger than the female and has an inflatable crest or 'hood'. Generally grey with irregular blotching.
Range This is a seal of the North Atlantic and Arctic seas, particularly around Bear Island, Spitzbergen and Jan Mayen Island, which is one of the main breeding areas. It is not uncommon off the Norway coast (and at least one pup has been born there). There are records as far south as the Bay of Biscay, the French/Spanish border and Portugal, but there are only about ten records from the British Isles over the last 150 years.
Habitat Thick drifting ice-floes in deep water, rarely firm ice.
Behaviour Rather solitary species, but forms small, loose aggregations of 'family' groups during the breeding season and larger concentrations in July and August during the moulting period.
Breeding Mating occurs at the end of a short lactation period of three to five days from March to April.
Food Thought to be able to dive to depths of greater than 180 m (580 ft), and to feed on fish (such as halibut, redfish, capelin and cod) and squid.

Harbour or Common Porpoise
Phocoena phocoena
Cetacea; Phocoenidae

Size 1.5–1.8 m (5–6 ft)
Weight 50–70 kg (100–150 lb)

Identification Smallest European cetacean. The body is short
and rotund, and the short, blunt head has no beak. The dorsal
fin is small, bluntly triangular and placed at the mid-point of
the back. The tail flukes are dark and have a median notch.

Range Temperate and subarctic waters of the North Atlantic,
including the Baltic Sea. It ranges from the White Sea to the
Mediterranean with many records from the Atlantic coasts of
southern and western Ireland, western Scotland and the
northern North Sea (particularly north-east of Scotland).
Habitat This is the most frequently seen and stranded
cetacean; it often enters estuaries and may travel considerable
distances up large rivers. Although generally a species of
coastal waters, usually being seen within 10 km (6 miles)
of land, it does venture further off-shore in winter.
Behaviour Most sightings are of solitary animals or of small
groups from July to October. It is a slow swimmer and rarely
breaches clear of the water.
Breeding Young are born from May to August.
Food Fish, crustaceans and cephalopods.
Conservation Now scarce in the Mediterranean and the
Black Sea through hunting, pollution and heavily exploitative
fisheries operations.

Long-finned Pilot Whale or Blackfish

Globicephala melas
Cetacea; Delphinidae

Size 4–8.5 m (13–28 ft)
Weight 1,800–3,500 kg (4,000–8,000 lb).

Identification Long and slender with a very bulbous head and a very short beak with the upper lip slightly protruding beyond the lower lip. Some white on underside and often elsewhere. Flippers long, slender and pointed.
Range Widespread in temperate waters: recorded from the Mediterranean and Iberia to the Faroes, Iceland and west of Norway. It is the most commonly observed species in Britain and Ireland, particularly western Ireland, north-western Scotland, Shetland and the Faroes. It is scarce in the southern end of the North Sea and the eastern reaches of the English Channel.
Habitat Seen mostly in off-shore pelagic waters, but also in coastal waters.
Behaviour It may be seen especially between November and January when there may be some inshore movement. It is gregarious, a slow swimmer, which seldom breaches, but may tail-smack. They frequently lie vertically in the water with the head and the top of the flippers exposed above the water.
Breeding More or less aseasonal.
Food Squid, cuttlefish and fish.
Conservation Fact of often travelling in large groups may mask seriously depleted populations.

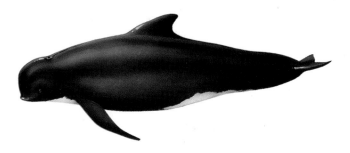

Killer Whale or Orca
Orca orca

Size 5.5–9.5 m (18–31 ft)
Weight 2.5–5 tonnes (2.75–5.5 tons)

Identification Deep torpedo-shaped body and a conical head with an indistinct beak. The striking black and white pattern varies. Flippers large and rounded. Tall, erect dorsal fin.
Range World-wide. In Europe it is most common around Iceland, the Faroes and western Norway. In Britain and Ireland it is mainly seen in west and northern Ireland, north-western Scotland, Orkney and Shetland and north-eastern England. It is scarce in the Baltic Sea, the eastern end of the English Channel, the southern end of the North Sea and south to the Mediterranean.

Habitat Cold coastal waters, but is probably more pelagic in winter.
Behaviour Recorded in coastal waters mainly from April to September. Usually solitary or in small groups. It is a very fast swimmer.
Breeding Most births are from October to January.
Food Fish, squid and other marine mammals, sometimes turtles and birds. It will occasionally eat carrion. Sometimes uses co-operative feeding techniques.
Conservation Not threatened.
Similar species The BASKING SHARK *Cetorhinus maximus* and other shark species show a similar-looking dorsal fin, but also show the tip of the vertical tail-fin.

Bottle-nosed Dolphin
Tursiops truncatus

Size 2.5–4 m (8–13 ft)
Weight 150–175 kg (300–400 lb)

Identification Stout, torpedo-shaped body with short beak
and lower jaw extending slightly beyond upper jaw. Dorsal fin
tall, slender and backwardly curved, dark or with a pale centre.
Tail flukes with curved margin and deep median notch.
Range World-wide except in very high latitudes.
Locally common in south Europe from the Black Sea and the
Mediterranean to western and northern Britain and Ireland,
and even to southern Norway.

Habitat Mainly found in coastal waters within 10 km
(6 miles) of the shore.
Behaviour Usually solitary or in small groups. They may be
seen in all months, but especially from July to September,
often associated with pilot whales in off-shore waters. A slow
swimmer, it frequently breaches clear of the water or stands
vertically with its head above the water surface. It will often
bow-ride ships or even large whales.
Breeding Peak number of births from March to May.
Food Fish, squid and cuttlefish.
Conservation Now scarce in much of the North Sea and the
Baltic Sea and considered threatened in the Black Sea and
much of the Mediterranean from hunting, incidental catching
in nets, pollution and competition with fishing industries.

Risso's Dolphin or Grampus
Grampus griseus

Size 3.3–3.8 m (10–12.5 ft)
Weight 350–400 kg (750–900 lb)

Identification Large, stout, torpedo-shaped body, blunt head with somewhat bulbous forehead and no beak, but a deep V-shaped furrow in the forehead. Tail flukes with concave rear margin and a median notch.
Range All tropical and temperate seas. In north-eastern Atlantic found from the Mediterranean to Scandinavia, particularly from western and northern Ireland, northern and western Scotland, Orkney and Shetland. Scarce in southern half of North Sea and eastern end of English Channel.
Habitat Probably largely pelagic with some seasonal movement towards the coast in late summer.
Behaviour Usually in groups of up to ten. Slow swimmer and occasionally associates with pilot whales or ships. Young animals will breach clear of the water, but older ones usually just slap the water surface with their flippers, tail flukes or flanks. Often remains vertical in the water with the head exposed.
Breeding Little known.
Food Cephalopods and some fish.
Similar species ROUGH-TOOTHED DOLPHIN *Steno bredanensis* is very small (to 2.5 m [8 ft]), spotted and with a distinct white beak. Recorded tropical Atlantic as far north as Mediterranean Sea, plus strandings from France and the Netherlands.
FALSE KILLER WHALE *Pseudorca crassidens*, a pelagic species of tropical and warm temperate oceans, is long and slender (4.5–6 m [14.5–20 ft]) with a small, rounded, blunt head and no beak. Mainly black, usually with a patch of grey or near-white on belly between the short and slender flippers. Mass strandings were reported from Britain in 1927, 1934 and 1935, and a few recent sightings between the Mediterranean and Scandinavia.

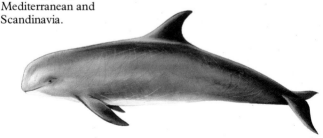

Common Dolphin
Delphinus delphis

Size 1.8–2.4 m (6–8 ft)
Weight 75–85 kg (165–185 lb)

Identification A slender, torpedo-shaped body with a long,
slender beak separated from its receding forehead by a groove.
The dorsal fin is large, slender and curved back, placed at
about midway along the back. Pattern variable, but normally
with more or less hour-glass pattern along flanks.
Range World-wide in temperate and tropical waters. Widely
distributed in British and Irish waters, but especially west and
south, scarce north of Ireland and east of Dorset. Occasionally
into the Baltic Sea and north to Norway and Iceland.
More common in the southern European Atlantic waters and
throughout the Mediterranean and Black Seas.
Habitat Mainly off-shore, and is particularly associated with
the western edges of the continental shelf and the Gulf Stream.
Behaviour Often gregarious. Most northern European
sightings are between July and October. It is a fast swimmer
and often follows ships to ride the bow wave. It frequently
breaches clear of the water and tail-smacks.
Breeding Births occur from June to September.
Food Pelagic fish and squid. Sometimes feeds co-operatively
by herding fish.

Conservation Populations depleted and heavily exploited in
some areas; the Mediterranean and Black Sea populations are
of special concern.
Similar species A number of distinct forms have been
recognized and are sometimes regarded as sub-species or
species.

Striped Dolphin
Stenella coeruleoabla

Size 2–2.7 m (6.5–9 ft)
Weight to 100 kg (220 lb)

Identification A torpedo-shaped body and an elongated beak, separated from the forehead by a distinct groove. Flanks variously marked with grey and longitudinal black lines. Dorsal fin long, slender, usually dark, placed about midway along the back. It frequently breaches clear of water and may bow-ride.

Range World-wide in tropical and warm temperate waters. Coasts of Spain, Portugal and France (plus one record from the Netherlands) and about twenty records from south-western Britain and Ireland. Also into the Mediterranean.
Behaviour Often gregarious, occurring in all months, especially from July to October and December to February. It is a fast swimmer and is often accompanied by common dolphins.
Breeding Births mainly from July to September.
Food Fish (such as anchovy or sardines) and squid with some crustaceans.
Conservation Mediterranean populations are threatened by hunting, drift-netting and pollution.
Similar species The eastern Mediterranean population has been proposed as a separate species.

Atlantic White-sided Dolphin
Lagenorhynchus acutus

Size 2–2.7 m (6–9 ft)
Weight to 165 kg (365 lb)

Identification A stout, torpedo-shaped body and a short beak.
Flanks grey with an elongated pale patch towards the rear
extended as a narrow yellowish band. The large, pointed sickle-
shaped dorsal fin is at the mid-point of the back. The tail stock
is very thick, and the tail flukes have a strongly concave margin
and slight median notch.

Range North Atlantic species. From central and western
Greenland, Iceland and the southern Barents Sea, south to
south-western Ireland and Cape Cod. The main concentrations
are off the Norwegian coast, north-western Scotland, Orkney,
Shetland and the Faroes. It is sometimes recorded in the Baltic
Sea, in the English Channel and the southern end of the North
Sea and in France.
Habitat Offshore, migrating between polar waters and
temperate waters.
Behaviour Most frequently seen in groups of less than ten
animals, but will form very large aggregations. A fast swimmer,
sometimes associated with pilot whales. It occasionally
breaches and bow-rides. Mostly seen between August and
October.
Breeding Most births from May to July.
Food Fish, some squid and gammarid crustaceans.

White-beaked Dolphin
Lagenorhynchus albirostris

Size 2.5–3 m (8–10 ft)
Weight up to 180 kg (400 lb)

Identification Stout, torpedo-shaped body with very short, light-coloured beak. Grey flank patch often extended over back towards rear of body. Large, erect, sickle-shaped dorsal fin situated about midway along back. Tail stock noticeably thick. Tail flukes dark with concave rear margin and slight median notch.

Range North Atlantic species. Found from central western Greenland and southern Barents Sea to Newfoundland, Cape Cod and south-western Ireland. Main European concentrations in Norway, western Ireland, north-western and northern Scotland, Orkney, Shetland and Faroes. Rarely recorded in Baltic and Irish Seas, the southern extremities of the North Seat and the English channel (including Brittany), plus once from Portugal.

Habitat More coastal than White-sided Dolphin.

Behaviour Recorded in most months, especially in August when there may be seasonal inshore movement. Most groups comprise less than ten animals. Fast swimmer, frequently approaches boats to bow-ride and breaches clear of the water.

Breeding Births mainly in May to August.

Food Fish, some squid, octopus and benthic crustaceans. Feeds co-operatively.

Similar species MELON-HEADED WHALE *Peponocephala electra*, a poorly known species of off-shore tropical and subtropical waters, is slender (2.3–2.7 m [7.5–8.5 ft]), with an indistinct beak. It is more or less all dark with paler belly. There is a single European record of a stranding in Cornwall, UK.

White Whale or Beluga
Delphinapterus leucas
Cetacea; Monodontidae

Size 3.5–5 m (11.5–16 ft)
Weight 500–1,500 kg (1,100–3,300 lb)

Identification The head is small with a bulbous forehead
(the 'melon') and a short beak. The adults are entirely white
making them unmistakable. Juvenile slate or reddish grey to
blue-grey. No dorsal fin; upper and lower jaws with eight to
eleven pairs of teeth.
Range Throughout the Arctic Ocean, only regularly seen as
far south as the northern Norway coast. Individuals recorded
in the Baltic Sea, in British coastal waters from Yorkshire north
around to south-western Ireland and from the North Sea coasts
of Denmark, Germany, the Netherlands and Belgium.

It is also recorded from France and possibly Spain.
Habitat Cold oceans and inshore waters, but occasionally
enters rivers.
Behaviour It is a relatively slow swimmer and a shallow diver.
It rarely breaches free of the water, but often beaches on sand
banks.
Breeding Young are born in the Arctic Ocean mainly in July
and August.
Food Mainly squid, also shallow-water fish and crustaceans.
Similar species None.

Narwhal
Monodon monoceros

Size 3.5–5.5 m (11.5–18 ft)
Weight 800–1,600 kg (1,700–3,500 lb)

Identification Similar in size and shape to white whale, but males (and sometimes females) have a unicorn-like spiralled tusk up to 3 m (10 ft) long. Body mottled green, paling with age. Tusk is one of a single pair of teeth in upper jaw; no teeth in lower jaw.

Range Throughout Arctic Ocean, sometimes in northern Norway's waters, but rarely into more temperate waters. Six records from British waters including into the North Sea as far as the Thames estuary (two records), but none reported for more than fifty years. Also recorded from the Netherlands and Germany.

Habitat Seems to prefer the deep water oceans and frequently follows pack-ice, but also comes into shallower waters.

Behaviour Fast swimmer. In temperate waters of our area records usually of individuals. In aggregations of up to 1,000 on migration.

Breeding Young born in summer.

Food Mainly squid and shallow-water, bottom-dwelling fish such as cod and halibut. Also some crustaceans (decapods and euphausiid shrimps).

Similar species Older individuals lacking tusk may be mistaken for White Whale *Delphinapterus leucas* (see page 103).

Sperm Whale
Physeter macrocephalus
Cetacea; Physetidae

Size females up to 10 m (30 ft); males up to 18 m (60 ft)
Weight up to 70 tonnes (77 tons)

Identification Massive squarish head making up almost
one-third of length. Short, slender lower jaws with complete
rows of teeth. Short round flippers. Small but distinct hump
on middle of back followed by smaller 'knuckles' along last
third of back. Blow conspicuous and 'bushy' (to about 2 m
[6.5 ft]), from front of head and directed towards the left.
Throws tail in air on diving.
Range Regular off north Norway to Spitzbergen, occasionally
off the Hebrides, Orkney, Shetland, western Ireland and
further south. Strandings reported rarely from Iberia to the
Netherlands. Recorded at all times of year and increasing.
Habitat Deeper waters of continental slope.
Behaviour Relatively slow swimmer, often solitary.
Breeding Single young may start to take solid food after
about one year, but female young may continue to suckle for
over seven years and males for up to thirteen years.
Food Squid but also fish.
Conservation Populations still depleted.
Similar species PYGMY SPERM WHALE *Kogia breviceps* less
than 4 m (13 ft), is more dolphin-like with a prominent dorsal
fin at the mid-point of the back, but with a rather large, blunt
head. Sightings and strandings from Atlantic coast of Ireland,
France and Portugal, and from the Netherlands and Italy.
DWARF SPERM WHALE *K. simus* is similar in size. It is recorded
as stranded once on French coast and sighted near entrance to
Mediterranean Sea.

Northern Bottle-nosed Whale
Hyperoodon ampullatus
Cetacea; Ziphiidae

Size 7–9.5 m(23–31 ft)
Weight 5–8 tonnes (5.75–9 tons)

Identification Head bulbous with short dolphin-like beak and
a pair of V-shaped throat grooves. Dorsal fin prominent, often
rather strongly hooked. Blow low (to 2 m 6.5 ft]) directed
slightly forward, and 'bushy'.
Range North Atlantic. Migrates late summer from Arctic to
warmer parts of northern Atlantic, returning for April to July.
Habitat Generally in deep waters (over 1,000 m [3,250 ft]),
but some inshore movement during migration. Most coastal
records from south-western approaches to Britain, the
Hebrides and northern North Sea and into the Baltic Sea.
Strandings recorded from Denmark, Belgium, England
and France.

Behaviour Usually solitary, sometimes in groups of up to ten
(or even fifty). Fast swimmer, often approaches vessels,
occasionally breaching or 'tail-lobbing'.
Breeding Young born April or May; lactation lasts for about
one year.
Food Squid, some fish and other invertebrates.
Conservation Evidence of continued decline in north-eastern
Atlantic Ocean.
Similar species CUVIER'S BEAKED WHALE *Ziphius cavirostris*, a
shy, pelagic species, grows to about 7 m (23 ft). Forehead
sloping, and weakly developed beak with slightly protruding,
pale lower jaw. Blow hole nearer snout, producing a low,
inconspicuous 'blow' directed forwards and slightly to the left.
Recorded rarely in northern waters from June to March from
western Ireland, northern and western Scotland, Orkney and
the Baltic, but much more common in southern Europe (Spain
and throughout the Mediterranean).

Sowerby's Beaked Whale
Mesoplodon bidens

Size 5–7 m (16–23 ft)
Weight up to 3.5 tonnes (4 tons)

Identification Long tapering body and small head with well-defined slender beak. Forehead with prominent bulge. One pair of teeth at mid-point of lower jaw of male.
Range Temperate North Atlantic, especially European waters. The main population centre is possibly around the North Sea.
Habitat Rarely seen and most knowledge is from strandings, particularly in the Faroes, Shetland, southern Scandinavia and countries bordering the North Sea to northern France. Rare in English Channel, western Ireland and western Scotland, but recorded from Bay of Biscay and two from the Basque coast.
Behaviour Said to be a fast swimmer, often at the surface, and usually solitary or in twos.
Breeding Believed to mate in the late winter and to give birth in the spring.
Food Mainly squid.
Similar species The genus *Mesoplodon* contains a number of very similar species, and a few other species have been recorded in Europe: TRUE'S BEAKED WHALE *M. mirus* is pale below, spotted above, grows to about 5 m (16 ft). Single pair of teeth at front of lower jaw. North Atlantic (east and west) and south to South Africa. Nine strandings in Europe, mostly from western Ireland, also outer Hebrides and France.
GRAY'S WHALE *M. grayi* is like Sowerby's whale but smaller (to 4.5 metres [14.5 ft]), lighter, teeth further forward. Southern Hemisphere species. One stranding in the Netherlands.
GERVAIS' or GULF STREAM WHALE *M. europaeus* is larger than Sowerby's (to more than 6 m [20 ft]), only slightly paler below, teeth just behind tip of jaw. North Atlantic species. Two strandings: Netherlands and north France.
BLAINVILLE'S WHALE *M. densirostris* is of medium size (to about 5 m [16 ft]), black above, grey below, single tooth in swollen posterior half of jaw. Tropical and warm temperate ocean to Madeira. One stranding in Spain.

Fin Whale or Common Rorqual

Balaenoptera physalis
Cetacea; Balaenopteridae

Size up to 24 m (78 ft)
Weight up to 80 tonnes (88 tons)

Identification Very slim with a narrow pointed head; almost uniform grey with distinct white area on lower lip and palate of right side. Blows with a single narrow cone about 4-6 m (13–20 ft) high, usually followed by a long shallow roll showing the flipper. Flukes rarely exposed when animal dives.
Range World-wide. Regular occurrences on migration off western coast of Europe, including from Ireland to the Baltic and western Norway. Also off Spain and into the western Mediterranean.
Habitat Primarily oceanic, but migrates along the continental shelf, especially from June to September. Rarely stranded on coasts, with six records from Britain between 1949 and 1987.
Behaviour Usually solitary, sometimes in herds of up to ten or twenty. Fast swimmer.
Breeding Births in warm temperate or subtropical waters between November and December.
Food Mainly crustaceans (euphausiid shrimps and copepods) and fish.
Conservation Formerly heavily exploited populations now showing some signs of recovery.
Similar species BLUE WHALE *B. musculus,* the largest whale (to about 30 m [100 ft]), is mottled pale blue grey. The very small dorsal fin is nearer the tail. Blow can reach to 9m (30 ft) and is vertical, tall and slender. Very occasional recorded off the north-eastern Atlantic continental shelf, recently off Ireland and Spain.

Minke Whale
Balaenoptera acutorostrata

Size up to 8.5 m (30 ft)
Weight up to 10 tonnes (11 tons)

Identification Like small fin whale with white patch on
upper surface of flippers. Dorsal fin taller, more sickle-shaped,
further forward. The tail flukes are broad with a small median
notch. The blow is low (to 2 m [6.5 ft]) and inconspicuous.
Occasionally breaches clear of the water.
Range World-wide in temperate and polar waters. Along the
European Atlantic seaboard of Ireland and Britain, Faroes,
western and northern Norway.

Habitat Often travels closer to the coast than other baleen
whales and has entered the Baltic Sea and the North Sea south
to Humberside and mid-Denmark.
Behaviour Mostly recorded between April and October,
especially August; usually solitary individuals, but sometimes
aggregations. A fast swimmer.
Breeding Peak birth period is December.
Food Fish, euphausiid crustaceans and pteropod squid.
Similar species SEI WHALE *B. borealis* grows to about 14.5 m
(47 ft), and is grey with a paler belly. The dorsal fin is slightly
further forward and more pointed. The blow is an inverted
cone to about 3 metres (10 ft). There are very few recent
recordswhich have come from off western Scotland, the Outer
Hebrides and the Netherlands.
BRYDE'S WHALE *B. edenii,* which is closely related, has also
been recorded.

Black (or Northern) Right Whale

Eubalaena glacialis
Cetacea; Balaenidae

Size 15–18 m (50–60 ft)
Weight 50–60 tonnes (55–66 tons)

Identification Head huge, to one-third of length, with strongly arched jaw. Head with distinct pale callosities. No dorsal fin. Tail flukes very broad with a concave trailing edge and a deep central notch. Blow shows two distinct spouts, rising to about 5 m (16 ft) in a V-shaped mist. Dives are vertical with tail flukes showing clear of water.
Range Cold and warm-temperate oceans of the northern hemisphere, now rare in the eastern Atlantic. Recent sightings in British and Irish waters (three), northern Spain (one), Madeira (one) and further out to sea.

Behaviour Most records from May to October, usually of solitary animals. Slow swimmer.
Breeding Single young born November to January.
Food Mainly copepods and euphausiid crustaceans.
Conservation Endangered.
Similar species BOWHEAD or GREENLAND RIGHT WHALE *Balaenoptera mysticetus* has even larger head and some white underneath. Unrecorded in European waters for many years. HUMPBACK WHALE *Megaptera novaeangliae* slimmer than the black, flippers one-third body length with irregular margins, throat grooved. Almost world-wide and migratory, but very rare now in eastern Atlantic (occasionally Iceland and the Azores). Sightings and strandings this century include Spain (three), France (three), British Isles (six) and some catches at the beginning of the century.

Domestic Horse

Equus caballus

Perissodactyla; Equidae

Size height at shoulder 1.2–1.5 m (4–5 ft);
tail to 0.5 m (1.5 ft)
Weight 270–390 kg (150–200 lb)

Identification Too familiar to need detailed description.
Long head, long slender legs with a single functional toe
bearing a large hoof, tail completely long-haired.
Range The ancestral tarpan ranged widely across Europe and
was last recorded in Europe in Poland in 1812. A number of
semi-natural populations similar to the wild type occur: for
example, in Exmoor in Britain. Feral populations of the extant
eastern race of the tarpan, Przewalski's horse, have been
established in France.
Habitat Moorland and rough grassland, usually with some
woodland cover.
Behaviour Feral horses usually live in small groups led by
a dominant male, but this harem structure is not always
maintained.
Breeding Most mating occurs in the early summer, gestation
takes about eleven months and the single young is suckled for
six to nine months.
Food A wide range of coarse herbaceous plants with a distinct
preference for grasses. In the autumn they browse on gorse
and trees, and will also eat moss and heather.
Conservation There are attempts to recreate the tarpan by
cross-breeding in Poland. Przewalski's horse is still very rare
in the wild (Mongolia), but well-established in captivity.

Domestic Donkey
Equus asinus

Size height at shoulders 1–1.4 m (3–4.5 ft);
tail to 0.5 m (1.5 ft)
Weight 250–370 kg (550–815 lb)

Identification Smaller than horses and have relatively longer ears, an erect mane and usually a dark stripe along the centre of the back and vertically down each shoulder. Long hair of tail restricted to outer half.

Range Throughout the region, but it probably originated from the African Ass *E. africanus* rather than the Wild Ass *E. hemionus* which occupied much of the desert and dry steppe zones from the Middle East to western Manchuria. There are few feral colonies in Europe: colonies in the south of Spain and Sardinia are examples.

Behaviour In the wild, donkeys live in small non-territorial groups, led by females, while the males hold large territories and mate with groups that enter their territory.

Breeding Usually one young (foal) born in the spring.

Food Primarily graze grass and herbaceous plants but do a lot more browsing than horses.

Wild Boar
Sus scrofa
Artiodactyla; Suidae

Size head & body 1.1–2 m (3.5–6.5 ft);
    tail 150–250 mm (6–10 ins)
Weight 135–230 kg (300–500 lb)

Identification Coat dense, bristly and grizzled, with underside woollier. The nostrils open on to a flat disc at the front of a snout which is generally longer than in domestic pigs. Males have well-developed tusk-like canines. Young have bold, longitudinal stripes of chestnut and yellowish brown.
Range Widespread in Europe to 60°N, with much reduced native populations and many re-introductions. Exterminated from Britain in about the seventeenth century. Absent from Ireland, most of Scandinavia, the extreme west of Europe and on and around the Alps. Present in Sardinia and Corsica.
Habitat Deciduous and mixed woodland to the treeline, often near lakes and marshland and ventures into pasture and arable land.
Behaviour More or less solitary, apart from a female accompanied by its young. Mainly nocturnal and dens in a shallow pit under a fallen tree or under rocks.
Breeding Mates between November and February, when the male may stay with the female and her young for several weeks. Most births, of two to ten young, occur from March to May.
Food Roots, tubers, fruits and nuts. Sometimes raids field crops and vineyards. Also takes rodents, young rabbits, birds' eggs, fish and amphibians, invertebrates and occasionally carrion.
Conservation Widely maintained for hunting.

Reeve's Muntjac
Muntiacus reevesi
Artiodactyla; Cervidae

Size head & body: 800–900 mm (30–36 ins);
tail 90–170 mm (3.5–6.75 ins)
Weight 9–18 kg (20–40 lb)

Identification A very small deer. The rounded back gives a
rather short-legged appearance. Rich red-brown above with a
buff belly and a conspicuous white underside to the short
broad tail. Tail often held vertically when alarmed. Male with
usually short and simple antlers and prominent upper canines.
Range Originating in south-eastern China (and Taiwan),
established in Britain from escapes since early this century.
Now expanding rapidly and occupies much of central and
southern England, with isolated populations in Wales and
Humberside.

Habitat Dense habitat with a diversity of vegetation, including
neglected coppice and gardens, pre-thinned plantation scrub,
and bramble thickets.
Behaviour Active mostly at dawn, midday and dusk, usually
solitary but sometimes aggregate.
Breeding More or less aseasonal with a 210-day pregnancy
and the single young being weaned at about seventeen weeks.
Food Bramble, ivy, ferns, fungi, a range of broad-leaved trees
and shrubs, nuts and other fruit.
Similar species CHINESE WATER DEER *Hydropotes inermis*,
with feral groups in Britain and France, has no antlers and no
facial markings, more rounded ears, a more upright stance and
a very inconspicuous, short brown tail.

Fallow Deer
Cervus dama

Size head & body 1.2 –1.6 m (4–5.25 ft);
tail 150–250 mm (6–10 ins)
Weight 35–120 kg (75–260 lb)

Identification Medium-sized deer typically reddish fawn with
white spots along the flanks and back and a black stripe along
the back. Greyer with spots less distinct in winter. Palmate
antlers (male) are shed from April to June and regrown by
September. Rump patch is white, edged with black. Tail white
with a broad black line extending full length of rump pattern.
Range Widely established from Mediterranean to about 61°N.
Most widespread species in Britain following re-introductions.
Habitat Mature woodland with established understorey and
adjacent grazing land.
Behaviour Diurnal where undisturbed, crepuscular elsewhere.
Generally the sexes separate for much of the year: males in
herds and hinds (females) in family groups which may
coalesce into herds.
Breeding Males compete to attract females during rut from
the end of September to November. Single young born in
June or July.
Food Grass, heather, broad-leaved browse, with seeds and
fruit in autumn and a range of browse in winter, including
bramble, holly, ivy, heather and conifers.
Similar species CHITAL or SPOTTED DEER *Cervus axis* has
been introduced to former Yugoslavia
and has escaped elsewhere. Antlers not
palmate and with no more than three
points. No black on the rump and
long tail.

Sika Deer
Cervus nippon

Size head & body 1–1.7 m (3–5.5 ft);
    tail 150–200 mm (6–8 ins)
Weight 36–84 kg (80–185 lb)

Identification Medium-sized, heavy, short-legged deer. Head relatively shorter, ears broader and more rounded than in red or fallow deer. Coat variable. White heart-shaped rump patch with a black stripe on the upper border. Tail white, sometimes with narrow black median stripe. Antlers well-branched, lowest branch angled less than 90° to main stem.
Range Widely introduced to Europe from eastern Asia (and Japan).There are park herds and scattered populations from escapees and introductions in the British Isles, particularly in Scotland, Ireland and south-west England.
Habitat Dense woodland, scrub and thicket stages of coniferous woodland. Visits open fields.
Behaviour Hinds form herds of forty to fifty or more. Active day and night.
Breeding Rut from end of September to early December. Males gather a harem of five to six animals. Single young born between May and early July.
Food Grasses and heathers, more browsing in winter. Also fungi and bark.
Similar species Sika/Red Deer hybrids cause identification problems. AMERICAN WHITE-TAILED DEER *Odocoileus virginianus* introduced to Bulgaria, the Czech Republic, Slovakia, Finland and former Yugoslavia, is unspotted with antlers arched forwards. The long tail, held erect and waved from side to side as the animal runs, is white underneath.

Red Deer
Cervus elaphus

Size head & body 1.2–2.1 m (4–7 ft);
  tail 150–190 mm (6–7.5 ins)
Weight 100–300 kg (220–660 lb)

Identification Large, generally uniform red-brown above with
a yellowish cream rump patch stretching from above level of
very short tail almost to ankle. Antlers (male) branched and not
deeply lined, the first point at 90° to main stem. Antlers shed
from February to April and regrown by August.
Range Widespread in Europe from 65°N in Norway to
Mediterranean and eastwards. In western Europe, Spain,
Corsica and Sardinia separate sub-species have been
recognized. Throughout Britain and Ireland, helped by
escapees and introductions; the Scottish highlands population
may be indigenous. North American (where called 'elk').
Habitat Open woodland and woodland edge, but, given
some cover, from semi-arid Mediterranean areas to the flood-
plains of the Danube, alpine meadows and in high snowfall
areas of Norway.
Behaviour For most of the year sexes in separate groups
of up to about forty, but sometimes several hundred.
Breeding Rut in September to November with stag
maintaining a harem. Single young born between May
and July.
Food Grasses, heather and small shrubs; also other herbs,
ferns, lichens and seaweed.
Sometimes browse on
deciduous trees in summer
and take bark in winter.
Similar species
Sika Deer
C. nippon.

Elk
Alces alces

Size head & body to 3 m (10 ft);
tail 120–130 mm (4.75–5 ins)
Weight 350–700 kg (770–1,540 lb)

Identification A very large deer, the size of a large horse.
Very long broad pendulous muzzle. Both sexes, but
particularly the male, have a well-furred dewlap from the throat
The male bears very large palmate antlers with up to twenty
points and a spread of up to 1.2 m (4 ft). They are shed
between November and January, regrown by July.
Range Scandinavia, Finland, north-eastern Poland and the
Baltic states and across most of the CIS and North America.
There may be relict isolated populations
in the south-west of Poland.

Habitat Coniferous woodland around water, but also in other
woodland and ranges on to mountains and into farmland in
search of food.
Behaviour Solitary, apart from in the rutting season, when
pairs are formed.
Breeding The rut lasts from the end of August to September
and sometimes October, with the young being born between
April and early June. Twins are frequent. The young usually
stay with the parents until the next birth.
Food Aquatic plants and shrubs; also shoots and bark of trees
and shrubs, ferns, lichens and fungi.

Reindeer
Rangifer tarandus

Size head & body to 2.2 m (7 ft);
  tail 100–150 mm (4–6 ins)
Weight 40–150 kg (90–350 lb)

Identification The fur colour is very variable, but usually
dark greyish brown in summer to almost white in winter. The
underparts are white. Old bulls have a distinct white mane in
winter. The hoofs are long and splayed, and the bones of the
foot produce a characteristic loud clicking as the animal walks.
Both sexes carry long, more or less palmate, antlers.
Range Scandinavia (but not southern Sweden) and Finland
east to the Bering Sea and north to Arctic Ocean islands. Also
found in North America ('caribou'). Much of the European
population now exists as domesticated herds or includes
animals of domestic origin. An introduced ranched population
thrives in the Cairngorms of Scotland.
Habitat Tundra of mountains or the Arctic, with some
populations migrating to coniferous forest edge in winter and,
in Finland, some herds are more permanently associated with
open woodland.
Behaviour Males mostly solitary; females form matriarchal
herds, which are joined by the males during the rut in
September and October.
Breeding One young (or occasionally twins) born between
April and June.
Food Lichens, supplemented
in summer with grasses,
sedges, heather and fungi.

Roe Deer
Capreolus capreolus

Size head & body 1–1.3 m (3–4 ft);
tail 20–40 mm (0.75–1.5 ins)
Weight 18–35 kg (40–77 lb)

Identification Small to medium-sized, more or less tail-less.
The almost circular cream-coloured rump patch is whiter in
winter. Antlers (male) are short, heavily ribbed and
tubercled with a well-developed coronet at the base; shed
October–January, regrown by March/April.
Range Through most of Europe north to lowland Scandinavia
and Finland except Mediterranean lowlands and islands. The
Siberian subspecies *C.c.pygargus*,
which some authorities regard as
a separate species, has been
widely introduced. In the
British Isles widespread,
mostly through
re-introductions, but absent
from much of central and
south-eastern England, Wales,
Ireland and most islands.
Habitat Open woodland, but
some populations use open
moorland or agricultural land.
Behaviour Mostly solitary or in
small family groups, but may
collect into groups of up to
twenty, or even sixty, in
winter.
Breeding The rut occurs
in July and August and is
more aggressive than in
most deer. The young are born in May
or June – twins are common.
Food Buds and shoots of deciduous trees and shrubs, herbs
and bramble, plus a range of other vegetation depending on
area and season.

Musk Ox
Ovibos moschatus
Artiodactyla; Bovidae

Size head & body 2–2.5 m (6.5–8 ft);
    tail 90–100 mm (3.5–4 ins)
Weight 225–400 kg (500–880 lb)

Identification Very robust, with distinctly hunched
shoulders. The extremely long and dense shaggy, dark outer
fur gives it a short-legged appearance. Very tightly curved
horns in both sexes.
Range Extinct in Europe since the last glaciation, the musk
ox is now only native to North America and Greenland, but
has been re-introduced to Norway (from where it has now
spread into Sweden) and to Spitzbergen.

Habitat Arctic tundra.
Behaviour Small groups of up to twelve in summer include
animals of both sexes. These groups link to form larger herds
of up to fifty in winter.
Breeding Mate between July and September and the single
young is born in May.
Food Grasses, sedges and dwarf shrubs and a range of other
tundra plants, such as *Vaccinium* and lichens.

Domestic Cattle
Bos taurus

Size height at shoulder 1 m (3 ft);
tail to 0.5 m (1.5 ft)
Weight up to 300 kg (660 lb)

Identification A great number of breeds have been
developed. One of the best documented, most pure-bred feral
breeds of long standing is the White Park Cattle of Chillingham
(Northumberland, England) whose general colouration is more
or less white with the inside of the ears dark (red) and the
naked part of the muzzle black. Both sexes horned.
Range Ubiquitous and common as a domestic animal. Apart
from the Chillingham herd, primitive feral cattle exist in the
Basque country of Spain, Scotland, Carmargue (France),
Corsica and Hungary.
Habitat Pasture with adjacent woodland is the preferred
natural habitat.
Behaviour The sexes remain in separate herds for much of
the year.
Breeding Aseasonal, although births are concentrated in
spring and summer.
Food Meadow grasses and herbs. The Swona Island herd
(Scotland) eats sea-weed as well as maritime heath.
Similar species The ancestor to the domestic cattle is the
Aurochs *Bos primigenus*, once widespread in Europe, Asia and
North Africa. Following destruction of forests and hunting, the
last European individual was killed in Poland in 1627. Extinct
in Britain for about 3,000 years. See also Bison *Bison bison*.

Bison
Bison bison

Size head & body 2.5–3.5 m (8–11.5 ft);
tail 600–800 mm (24–32 ins)
Weight 500–900 kg (1,000–2,000 lb)

Identification Head and forequarters particularly large and
strong and hind quarters slimmer and lower. Heavy mane on
neck and forequarters, especially in the bull. Horns short and
tightly curved inwards.
Range Once found throughout central Europe north to
southern Sweden and east to the Caucasus. It became extinct
in the wild in the 1920s, but some were held in captivity in
Poland. Re-introductions were made in 1952 and later years
to Poland and parts of European Russia (including the
Caucasus). The buffalo of North America is regarded by
many as the
same species.

Habitat Extensive mixed primeval forest with damp clearings.
Behaviour Males usually solitary; females and young in small
herds of up to twenty.
Breeding Rut between August and October and a single
young (sometimes twins) born between May and July.
Food Herbs, sedges, grasses, leaves and bark of trees and
shrubs. Autumn fruits, especially acorns, are sought; heathers
and evergreen eaten in winter.
Conservation Intensive conservation programmes have
resulted in several viable wild populations.
Similar species The domestic WATER BUFFALO *Bubalus
bubalis*, used in parts of southern Europe (notably Italy), is
uniform dark grey with flattened, evenly swept-back horns.

Alpine Chamois
Rupicapra rupicapra

Size head & body 1–1.3 m (3–4.25 ft);
tail about 150 mm (6 ins)
Weight 25–50 kg (55–110 lb)

Identification Small, slender, goat-like animal with a
distinctive pale rump patch. Horns in both sexes, short, very
close-set and upright with short, sharply backward-curved tip.
Black-and-white facial markings.
Range Fragmented montane populations in the Alps, the Jura,
Abruzzi (in Italy), the Carpathians, Tatra and Balkan
mountains, the Caucasus, the north of Asia Minor and the
Taurus Mountains. The populations of north-western Spain
and the Pyrenees are usually now regarded as a separate
species, the Pyrenean Chamois *R. pyrenaica*.
Habitat Upper limits of montane forest and higher open
slopes in extremely precipitous, rocky terrain. Descends to
woodland in winter.
Behaviour Most active at dawn and dusk. Mature males are
more or less solitary; females in groups of up to about fifteen
or more, but more solitary in winter.
Breeding The rut occurs in November and December, and
the single young, sometimes two, is born in May or June.
Food Mainly grazing
but also browsing
on wide variety of
plants, including
conifers, lichen
and bark in winter.
Conservation
Some sub-species (or
species), for example
in the Balkans, are
threatened.

Alpine Ibex
Capra ibex

Size head & body 1.3–1.5 m (4.25–5 ft)
   tail 120–150 mm (4.75–6 ins)
Weight 50–120 kg (110–265 lb)

Identification Like a stocky goat. Horns of male very large and evenly curved backwards with prominent closely-set ribs across a broad flat front. Female horns short.
Range Alps.
Habitat From above the treeline to the snow line, on steep rocks.
Behaviour Females and young form small herds in summer. Males solitary or form small groups, sometimes to twenty or thirty, often at higher altitudes than females. Extremely agile and sure-footed.
Breeding Rut between late November and January. Single young, sometimes twins, born May or June.
Food Alpine plants, including grasses, sedges, shrubs and lichens.
Conservation Was reduced to one national park in Italy, now widely re-established in Alps.
Similar species WILD GOAT *C. aegagrus:* found on some Aegean islands (sub-species *C. a. picta)*, including Crete (sub-species *cretica*) and, by introduction of latter, on Greek mainland. Horns smoothly curved backwards with sharp keel on front margin and poorly developed widely spaced ribs.
DOMESTIC GOAT *C. hircus*: feral colonies established in Europe in hilly or mountain areas or on islands. Often piebald with very long shaggy fur.
SPANISH IBEX *C. pyrenaica*: horns more distinctly twisted outwards and upwards and less prominently ribbed. Small isolated populations, many severely threatened, in Spanish Pyrenees and central Spain.

Mouflon
Ovis orientalis

Size head & body 1–1.3 m (3–4.25 ft),
tail 40–100 mm (1.5–4 ins)
Weight 25–50 kg (55–110 lb)

Identification A sheep with the short 'wool' outgrown by
some longer hairs. Mature males have reddish fur with a pale
patch on flanks and rump. Horns of male large, smoothly
curved towards a circle, markedly ringed.
Range Indigenous to the mountains of Iran and Asia Minor.
Descendants of early domestications were introduced to
Cyprus, Corsica and Sardinia, and from
Corsica and Sardinia to much of
central Europe, southern Spain and
the Pyrenees.

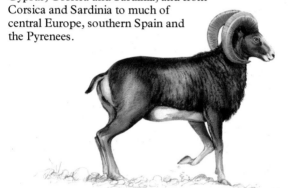

Habitat Mountainous open woodland with grassland.
Behaviour Often mainly nocturnal, laying up by day in thick
cover, but more diurnal in some areas, e.g. Poland. Males in
flocks, except in the rut; females in matriarchal flocks.
Breeding One or two young born between end of March and
early May.
Food Grasses, sedges and heaths, supplemented in winter by
browsing on leaves, twigs and bark.
Conservation Natural populations of Corsica and Sardinia
need protection.
Similar species Populations of Corsica and Sardinia are now
regarded as a separate subspecies (or even species), *O. o.
musimon*, distinct from the Cyprus population, *O. o. ophion*.
The DOMESTIC SHEEP (*O. aries*) is regarded as a descendant of
this species; feral colonies exist on some mountains and islands,
such as the St Kilda group off western Scotland.

European Rabbit

Oryctolagus cuniculus
Lagomorpha; Leporidae

Size head & body 340–450 mm (13.5–18 ins);
   tail 40–80 mm (1.5–3.25 ins)
Weight 1.2–2.2 kg (2.25–4.5 lb)

Identification Smaller than the hare, with relatively shorter
legs and ears and no distinct black tips to ears. Characteristic
hopping gait, and when running the tail is usually held up,
showing white underside.
Range Widespread in Britain and Ireland and on most small
islands, where it was introduced in twelfth century. Originates
from Iberia and southern France, but has spread and been
introduced to most of western Europe. Absent from Italy and
the Balkans.
Habitat Grassland, dry heaths, machair, agricultural pasture,
broad forest rides and clearings, dunes and sea cliffs.
Behaviour Social groups live in complex shared burrow
system. Mainly crepuscular or nocturnal, but frequently
diurnal when not disturbed.
Breeding There can be about six litters of about four young
a year between January and August.
Food Young leaves and shoots of grasses, agricultural crops,
bark and twigs.
Conservation Widely regarded as a pest.
Similar species COTTON-TAIL RABBITS (*Sylvilagus floridianus*
and *S. transitionalis*) have been
introduced to parts of Europe
from North America: both are
solitary and have shorter ears
and tail.

Arctic (Mountain) Hare
Lepus timidus

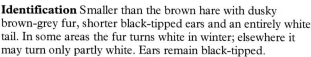

Size head & body 450–600 mm (18–24 ins);
 tail 40–85 mm (1.5–3.25 ins)
Weight 1.7–5.8 kg (3.75–12.75 lb)

Identification Smaller than the brown hare with dusky
brown-grey fur, shorter black-tipped ears and an entirely white
tail. In some areas the fur turns white in winter; elsewhere it
may turn only partly white. Ears remain black-tipped.
Range Ireland, Scotland (except the east and south-west) and
just into north-eastern England, with isolated populations in
Derbyshire and the Isle of Man. On mainland Europe it occurs
through tundra and coniferous forest zone from Scandinavia to
eastern Siberia and in the Alps and Pyrenees.
Habitat Upland heather moorland and grassland but also
open woodland in winter. Occurs down to sea level where the
brown hare is absent (as in Ireland).
Behaviour More social than the brown hare, often forming
quite large groups but not colonies. Lays up in heather,
shallow scrapes, among boulders. Sometimes digs a short,
simple burrow. In snow, they make shallow scrapes or
tunnel to known burrows.
Breeding Makes heather-lined nests in mature heather and
commonly have three litters of one to four young per year.
Food Prefers young heather and grasses, but also takes older
heather, rushes, sedges, lichens, bark and twigs, cereal and
root crops.
Similar species Rabbit *Oryctolagus cuniculus* (see page 127)
and Brown Hare *L. capensis*.

Brown Hare
Lepus capensis

Size head & body 480–680 mm (19–27 ins);
 tail 80–120 mm (3–5 ins)
Weight 2.5–6.5 kg (5.5–14.5 lb)

Identification The largest species with rich yellow-brown fur and long black-tipped ears. The belly and underside of the tail are white, and the upper surface of the tail is black. In winter the body fur is redder with a greyer rump. It has a longer body than the rabbit and relatively longer legs, giving it its characteristic loping gait.
Range Throughout mainland Britain, except north-western Scotland, on major offshore islands and introduced into parts of Ireland. On mainland Europe, it occurs from southern Sweden and Finland to the Mediterranean, on most major Mediterranean islands and eastwards across most of CIS.
Habitat Open woodland, steppe, sub-desert, dunes and farm land.
Behaviour More or less solitary, but often occurs in loose aggregations. Characteristic 'boxing' behaviour, rearing up in face-to-face contest, is usually between males and non-receptive females.
Breeding Rear young in shallow depression ('form'). Generally three litters of one to four young between February and October.
Food Grasses, herbs and cereal crops in summer; in winter, bark and twigs and root crops.
Conservation Declined in some areas due to changes in farming methods.
Similar species Arctic Hare *L. timidus* has shorter black-tipped ears and greyer (or white) fur.

Red Squirrel
Sciurus vulgaris
Rodentia; Sciuridae

Size head & body 180–250 mm (7–10 ins);
    tail 140–220 mm (5.5–9 ins)
Weight 220–450 g (0.5–1 lb)

Identification Dorsal fur usually uniform red or chestnut;
grey or black in some seasons and regions. Ventral fur is pale.
Ears bear obvious tufts in winter.
Range Widely distributed in Europe from the Mediterranean
to north of the Arctic circle. Still widespread in central and
southern Scotland but only relict populations in England
and Wales.
Habitat Deciduous and coniferous woodland to 2,000 m
(6,500 ft).

Behaviour Mostly solitary, although some communal nesting
in winter. Remains inactive for several days during severe
weather. Mainly arboreal and builds dreys near the tree trunk
at least 6m (20ft) above ground.
Breeding Up to three litters of three to four young between
February and August.
Food Tree seeds, fruit, berries and fungi. Buds, shoots, flowers
and bark are also eaten and sometimes other green matter,
invertebrates and lichens. In autumn, seeds are cached
underground and fungi in trees.
Conservation Declining in Britain due to a loss of habitat and
competition with the introduced grey squirrel.
Similar species *S. anomalus* is slightly smaller, with no ear
tufts and yellowish-buff ventral fur. Occurs on Lesbos
(Greece) and in Turkey.

Grey Squirrel
Sciurus carolinensis

Size head & body 240–300 mm (9.5–12 ins);
tail 195–240 mm (7.75–9.5 ins)
Weight 400–700 g (14–25 oz)

Identification Upper fur is mainly grey with some brown on back, and on flanks and legs in summer. No conspicuous ear tufts.
Range Introduced into the British Isles from eastern North America.
Habitat Mature broad-leaved woodland, but also found in mixed woodland, hedgerows, parks and gardens.
Behaviour Mainly solitary, but may nest communally in winter. Spends more time on the ground than the red squirrel. Summer dreys are usually a platform of twigs, while the winter nests are more substantial, like those of the red squirrel.
Breeding Breeds in dreys or tree-holes and one or two litters of two to four young are born between February and July.
Food Mainly seeds and fruit of deciduous trees and shrubs, but also coniferous seeds. It caches seeds underground in autumn. In spring and summer, feeds on flowers and buds, but also eats bark and occasionally fungi, invertebrates, birds' eggs and nestlings.
Conservation Often regarded as a pest.
Similar species Can be distinguished from the Red Squirrel *S. vulgaris* by size, colour and lack of conspicuous ear tufts.

Siberian Chipmunk
Tamias sibiricus

Size head & body 150–220 mm (6–9 ins);
tail 100–140 mm (4–5.5 ins)
Weight 50–120 g (2–4.5 oz)

Identification Tail is shorter and less bushy than in tree
squirrels, but much longer and bushier than in sousliks. Fur is
warm brown above, pale below, with a dark dorsal stripe from
shoulders to base of tail and two similar stripes on each side of
the body. There are dark markings on the face.

Range Siberian taiga (conifer forest) as far west as
White Sea. Introduced in France, Germany, the Netherlands
and Austria.
Habitat Bushy undergrowth of open woodland.
Behaviour Active by day on ground and in shrubs and
small trees. Does not truly hibernate. Nests in burrows or
hollow logs.
Breeding Poorly known in Europe but probably one or
two litters of four or more young.
Food Nuts and other seeds, which it hoards in large
quantities in autumn.

Alpine Marmot
Marmota marmota

Size head & body 500–580 mm (20–23 ins);
tail 140–190 mm (5.5–7.5 ins)
Weight 3.5–7 kg (7.75–15.5 lb)

Identification Heavy, compact body, short legs and rolling gait. Fur is coarse, grey-yellow above, darker on the midline of the back and paler underneath. Top of head is dark brown or black and tip of muzzle and feet are yellow-white. Tail is less than half the body length and is well-haired and black-tipped.
Range Native to the Alps, Carpathian and Tatra mountains, but introduced in the Massif Central (France), the central Pyrenees and northern former Yugoslavia.
Habitat Alpine pastures and rocky hillsides, mainly above the treeline to 3,000 m (9,750 ft).
Behaviour Lives in family groups in burrows. Diurnal, often sitting up on haunches to watch for predators. Hibernates from October to April.
Breeding Single litter of two to six young born towards the end of June.
Food Grasses, sedges and other herbaceous plants, and occasionally roots.
Similar species STEPPE MARMOT *M. bobak* is of similar size, but the colour of the face and neck is not clearly different from the crown and nape. Its westerly limits are now the steppes of southern Russia and Kazakhstan, although it used to occur in Poland, Romania and Hungary.

European Souslik
Spermophilus citellus

Size head & body 190–230 mm (7.5–9 ins);
   tail 55–80 mm (2.25–3.25 ins)
Weight 175–340 g (6–12 oz)

Identification Upper parts greyish yellow, throat white and belly yellowish grey. Back is uniform to faintly mottled. Eyes large and ears short. The tail is one-quarter to one-third of the head and body length, well-furred and marked with obscure black and white zones.
Range From south-eastern Germany and south-western Poland to eastern former Yugoslavia and northern Greece and east to Romania and beyond.
Habitat Dry grassland, including man-made pasture and edges of cultivated land, road and rail embankments to 2,500 m (8,125 ft).
Behaviour Colonial in burrow. Diurnal and frequently sit upright in squirrel-like fashion when looking out for predators. Hibernates in some areas in winter and may sleep for extended periods in dry summers.
Breeding Single litter of about six young born in May to June.
Food Mainly seeds, which are stored in autumn, and green vegetation. Some insects are also eaten.
Conservation Declining.
Similar species
Spotted Souslik
S. suslicus.

Spotted Souslik
Spermophilus suslicus

Size head & body 180–250 mm (7–10 ins);
     tail 25–50 mm (1–2 ins)
Weight 170–375 g (6–13 oz)

Identification Differs from European souslik in having
obvious pale spots on yellowish grey to dark brown fur on
back, a less hairy and shorter tail (about 20 per cent of head

and body length). Belly greyish red or greyish yellow with
lighter patches on the breast and neck.
Range Southern part of European Russia west of rivers Volga
and Don to south-eastern Poland and north-eastern Romania.
Habitat Grassy steppes and cultivated ground.
Behaviour Similar to European souslik, but may form larger
colonies, particularly around cultivated areas, where its deeper
burrows may allow it to survive ploughing. Hibernates between
October and early April.
Breeding Single litter of four to seven young born in May to
early June.
Food Mainly green vegetation and seeds but also invertebrates.
Similar species European Souslik *S. citellus*.

Russian Flying Squirrel
Pteromys volans

Size head & body 140–200 mm (5.5–8 ins);
　　tail 90–140 mm (3.5–5.5 ins)
Weight 95–180 g (4–6 oz).

Identification Small, pale grey, slender squirrel with large eyes, short rounded ears and a flattened tail. A gliding membrane extends from wrist to ankle but is inconspicuous when not in use, and the animal might be mistaken for a fat dormouse.
Range Finland and around the Baltic coast almost to Poland. Occurs southwards to 50° N in the east.

Habitat Deciduous or coniferous forests, particularly where there is mature birch.
Behaviour Nocturnal and almost exclusively arboreal, gliding from tree to tree. It nests in tree holes and does not hibernate.
Breeding Two litters of two to three young are born in April to May and June to July.
Food Seeds, nuts, berries, buds, shoots, leaves and fungi, with occasionally birds' eggs and fledglings. Food cached for winter includes catkins and twigs.
Conservation Rare and declining, especially in Finland.
Similar species Fat dormouse *Glis glis* (see page 172).

Eurasian Beaver
Castor fiber
Rodentia; Castoridae

Size head & body 750–1000 mm (30–40 ins);
    tail 250–400 mm (10–16 ins)
Weight 9–30 kg (20–66 lb)

Identification The most distinctive feature is the broad, flat, scaly tail. Webbed hind feet.
Range Formerly throughout the forested zone, but now only on parts of the rivers Rhône and Elbe and in southern Norway. Being returned to parts of Europe, and in Britain some temporary feral colonies have formed from escaped captives.
Habitat Riverine forest, particularly with aspen, birch and other broad-leaved trees, and around lakes and swamps.
Behaviour Graceful swimmer. Mainly nocturnal and lives in small, territorial family groups in unobtrusive riverside burrows with the entrance below water level. In Europe seldom builds dams and lodges.
Breeding Litters of two to four young born in late spring. Young may stay with adults for more than a year.
Food Vegetable matter in summer including tree bark and cambium, shoots, roots and aquatic plants. In winter, concentrates on bark and twigs.
Conservation Being re-introduced in some parts of Europe.
Similar species The WESTERN BEAVER has had the name *C. albica* applied to it. CANADIAN BEAVER *C. canadensis* is slightly smaller with a darker head and shorter muzzle; it has been introduced to parts of Finland, Scandinavia and Germany and may hybridize.

European Hamster
Cricetus cricetus
Rodentia; Muridae

Size head & body 200–300 mm (8–12 ins)
tail 30–65 mm (1.25–2.5 ins)
Weight 250–650 g (9–23 oz)

Identification Unusual in having underside fur darker than upper fur, which is usually yellowish brown with a pattern of darker (reddish) or paler (white or yellowish white) patches. The tail is very short with no tuft at tip.

Range Widespread in eastern and central Europe with small, scattered populations in Belgium, the Netherlands and northern France.
Habitat Open steppe and grasslands to about 500 m (1,625 ft).
Behaviour Solitary but aggregate in suitable habitat. Active mainly around dawn and dusk. Digs deep burrows with nesting and food storage chambers. Hibernates for short periods throughout winter. When alarmed, it inflates its cheek pouches and jumps to about 1 m (3 ft).
Breeding Two or three litters of six to twelve young may be born between April and August.
Food Omnivorous: wide range of plant material, insects, worms, snails and even small vertebrates. Stores food for winter, often in large quantities of up to 65 kg (150 lb).
Conservation In need of strict protection.
Similar species Other hamsters, and the introduced GUINEA PIG *Cavia porcellus*.

Grey Hamster
Cricetulus migratorius

Size head & body 90–120 mm (3.5–4.75 ins);
tail 15–30 mm (0.5–1.25 ins)
Weight 25–35 g (1–1.5 oz)

Identification Rather vole-like but with larger ears and eyes
and a shorter tail. Plain grey-brown above, very pale below.
Range Scattered localities in the Balkans including parts of
Bulgaria, Greece and Romania, and from Turkey and
southern parts of the European CIS eastwards to Mongolia,
north to Moscow and south to the Middle East, Iran and
Afghanistan.
Habitat Cultivated and natural grassland, also in open
woodland.
Behaviour Principally nocturnal and lives in its own burrow
close to other members of the species. Probably hibernates in
severe weather.
Breeding May have two to three litters of five to six young
per year.
Food Buds, leaves, nuts and seeds. More vegetarian than
other hamsters, but does take some invertebrates. Stores
surplus food in burrows for winter.
Similar species Much smaller than the European Hamster
C. cricetus without dark markings.

Romanian Hamster
Mesocricetus newtoni

Size head & body 150–180 mm (6–7.25 ins);
    tail 10–20 mm (0.5–0.75 ins)
Weight 80–150 g (3–5 oz)

Identification Upper fur pale yellowish brown, pale underside with black chest spot or band and elongate dark patch on side of neck that may extend across chest. Dark patches on nape and around eyes. Short tail.
Range Lowlands of eastern Romania, Bulgaria and the Ukraine around the Black Sea.
Habitat Steppes and agricultural land.
Behaviour Mainly nocturnal. Each individual in an aggregation of animals defends its own burrow.
Breeding One or two litters of up to twelve young born from early summer to early autumn.
Food Mainly seeds, roots, young shoots and some invertebrates.
Similar species GOLDEN HAMSTER *M. auratus,* from Asia Minor to the Caucasus and Kurdistan, is of similar size and has a barely visible tail. This widely kept domestic animal is very variable in colour. It has escaped and formed feral colonies in many parts of Europe.

Wood Lemming
Myopus schisticolor

Size head & body 85–100 mm (3.25–4 ins);
　　　tail 15–20 mm (0.5–0.75 ins)
Weight up to 45 g (2 oz)

Identification Uniform slaty grey, becoming paler in winter, but with very short russet tail and inconspicuous russet streak or patch on rump. Ears very short.

Range Norway, Sweden, Finland, and through most of northern Siberia.
Habitat Coniferous forest, especially spruce and wet sphagnum moss with secondary growth. Sometimes in tundra.
Behaviour Makes burrows and runways in moss. Largely nocturnal.
Breeding May produce two litters of three to seven young between June and August, but may breed almost all year in some parts of range. Many females produce only female young. Populations fluctuate but not as wildly as Norway lemming.
Food Mosses, also liverworts and lichens.
Similar species The Northern Red-backed Vole *Clethrionomys rutilus* (see page 144) has a longer tail, is more rufous on the back and paler below.

Norway Lemming
Lemmus lemmus

Size head & body 130–150 mm (5–6 ins);
tail 15–20 mm (0.5–0.75 ins)
Weight up to 130 g (5 oz)

Identification Compact with very short ears and tail. Fur
conspicuously patterned in black, yellow-orange and white.
Range Alpine zones of mountains of Scandinavia and on
tundra from Lapland east to the White Sea. Probably part of
one circumpolar species.
Habitat Tundra and open birch/willow scrub, also woodland
and cultivation in 'lemming years'.
Behaviour Lives in shallow burrows in summer and runways
under snow in winter, which leave tracings when snow melts.
Breeding Mostly in summer, but might continue into winter,
and a female may then bear up to six litters in a year. Litter size
varies between two and thirteen but is usually four to eight.
'Lemming years' occur about every four years and sometimes
reach 'plague' proportions when mass emigrations occur.
At this time the aggregations have no social structure and the
individuals are very aggressive.
Food Grasses, sedges, dwarf shrubs, mosses, lichens and fungi.
Similar species ARCTIC LEMMING *Dicrostonyx torquatus* of
the Siberian tundra west to the White Sea, is similar and
appears to be spreading westwards. It develops large flat claws
in winter.

Bank Vole
Clethrionomys glareolus

Size head & body 65–110 mm (2.5–4.25 ins);
tail 30–60 mm (1.25–2.25 ins)
Weight 16–35 g (0.75–1.25 oz)

Identification Typical vole with blunt nose, small eyes and relatively short tail. Ears are also small but visible above fur. Reddish chestnut back, greyer flanks and pale grey underside.

Tail equals 40–60 per cent of the length of head and body.
Range From Arctic Circle in Scandinavia to northern Spain, northern Italy and the Balkans (except most of Greece), east to Lake Baikal and northern Kazakhstan. In Britain, it is found on mainland Britain and many islands, with separate sub-species on the islands of Jersey, Skomer (Wales), Mull and Raasay. Recently introduced in Ireland.
Habitat Mature, mixed deciduous woodland with thick scrub or herb layer, also coniferous woodland, hedgerows and occasionally grasslands up to 2,400 m (7,800 ft).
Behaviour Active day and night, making runways on ground surface or under ground.
Breeding May produce litters of four to seven at intervals of three to four weeks between March and October.
Food Fruits, seeds, buds and leaves, fungi, lichens, mosses, roots, flowers and grasses. Occasionally eats bark and dead leaves in winter, caches food and eats its own fresh droppings (refection). Occasionally eats insects and worms.
Similar species Other Red-backed Voles (*Clethrionomys* species, see page 144–145).

Northern Red-backed Vole
Clethrionomys rutilus

Size head body 80–100 mm (3.25–4 ins);
     tail 25–35 mm (1–1.25 ins)
Weight 15–40 g (0.5–1.5 oz)

Identification Lighter and brighter rufous colour above and
paler below than bank vole. Tail particularly short with
terminal tuft.
Range Tundra and taiga forest zone of northern Scandinavia
and Finland south to about 60°N, but also eastwards to Siberia
and Japan, south to 45°N in central Asia and
in arctic North America.

Habitat Open alpine birch woodland and widow scrub,
sometimes coniferous forest. Frequently enters buildings in
winter.
Behaviour Active day and night (more nocturnal in summer).
Usually nests in burrows, in other surface structures or
sometimes above ground in trees. An agile climber.
Breeding May have three or four litters of about seven young
each year.
Food Seeds and berries, often collected from bushes and low
trees.
Similar species Other Red-backed Voles (*Clethrionomys*
species, see page 143, 145).

Grey-sided Vole
Clethrionomys rufocanus

Size head & body 100–130 mm (4–5 ins);
tail 25–40 mm (1–1.5 ins)
Weight up to 50 g (2 oz)

Identification Differs from bank vole and northern red-backed vole in being a larger size and in having the rufous colouring restricted to almost a band along the top of the back, contrasting with distinctly grey flanks. Tail is still relatively short, but proportionately longer than other species.
Range From Scandinavia and Finland through Siberia to the Pacific coast and Japan. In Scandinavia comes further south than the northern red-backed vole on the central mountain chain.
Habitat Tundra, but also in open birch/pine woodland and in heathland areas on mountains.
Behaviour An able climber.
Breeding Has up to four litters of about six young each year. Young may breed in their first year.
Food Shoots of dwarf shrubs such as bilberry, crowberry, and leaves and bark of shrubs and low-growing trees.
Similar species Other Red-backed Voles (*Clethrionomys* species, see pages 143–144).

Martino's Snow Vole
Dinaromys bogdanovi

Size head & body 100–140 mm (4–5.5 ins);
tail 70–110 mm (2.75–4.25 ins)
Weight 50–80 g (2–2.75 oz)

Identification Fur long and soft, pale grey above and white below. Tail relatively long. Ears quite prominent, hind feet fairly large and tail about three-quarters the combined length of the head and body.
Range Mountains of former Yugoslavia and probably northern Albania.
Habitat Rocky slopes above tree-line at 600–2,000 m (2,000–6,500 ft), usually in grassland but sometimes in woodland.
Behaviour Little known, but active at all times of day and night. Makes nest in rock crevice or in short burrow under stones.
Breeding Usually two litters of two to three, one from March to April and one from June to July.
Food Grasses, some roots and probably other plant material, some of which is stored for winter.
Conservation Rarely seen and little studied.
Similar species Snow Vole *Microtus nivalis* (see page 152) has a relatively shorter tail and smaller feet, and has not been recorded from the Balkans.

Northern Water Vole
Arvicola terrestris

Size head & body 120–260 mm (4.75–10.25 ins);
    tail 70–170 mm (2.75–6.75 ins)
Weight 200–380 g (7–13.5 oz)

Identification A large but typical vole, although tail is 55–70
per cent of head-body length. Dorsal fur is reddish to medium
dark brown, even almost black, with paler ventral fur.
Range From the edge of the Arctic to the Mediterranean, but
absent from most of western France, Iberia, southern Balkans
and most Mediterranean islands. Found throughout mainland
Britain except north and north-western Scotland; absent from
most islands and Ireland.

Habitat Densely vegetated banks of slow-moving rivers and
ponds. Also lives away from water, where it sometimes leads a
very subterranean life.
Behaviour Females fairly solitary and territorial, but may have
communal nests. Males have a large range and are not very
territorial. A little more active in daytime than at night. Nest is
usually underground in complex burrow system. Swims well.
Breeding Up to five litters of three to six young born between
April and October.
Food Grasses, sedges, rushes and some dicotyledonous plants.
In winter it includes rhizomes and roots and hay stored
underground in autumn. Rarely takes insects, molluscs and fish.
Conservation Marked decline in some areas due to river
management and introduced pests.
Similar species SOUTHERN WATER VOLE *A. sapidus* of Iberia
and western France is larger, darker and longer-tailed than
southern population of northern water vole.

Muskrat
Ondatra zibethicus

Size head & body 270–400 mm (11–16 ins);
  tail 200–280 mm (8–11 ins)
Weight 750–1450 g (2–3 lb)

Identification Very large aquatic vole with long, laterally
compressed naked tail, thick, soft fur and very short ears. Fur
dark brown with russet tinge. Hind feet with fringe of dense
bristles.
Range Introduced from North America for its fur and has
occurred in much of central and northern Europe. No
populations currently in the British Isles.
Habitat Near stagnant or slow-moving water of rivers, lakes,
ponds and marshes with well vegetated banks.
Behaviour Aquatic and able to swim long distances under
water, usually surfacing in cover. Especially active in the early
morning. Makes dens in banks with entrances below water.
Builds domed dens as temporary resting places or food stores
on water surface in winter. Does not hibernate.
Breeding Three or four litters of four to eight young each
year. More or less monogamous.
Food Aquatic plants supplemented with molluscs, and by
rhizomes and crop plants in winter.
Similar species Other aquatic rodents are either smaller (Rats
and Water Voles, see pages 163–164 and 147) or larger
(Coypu and Beaver, see pages 178 and 137). Their tails are
distinctly different, but these are rarely seen while the animals
are swimming.

European Pine Vole
Pitymys subterraneus

Size head & body 75–115 mm (3–4.5 ins);
    tail 20–40 mm (0.75–1.5 ins)
Weight 11–24 g (0.5–1 oz)

Identification Similar to grass voles (*Microtus* species), but
with even smaller eyes, ears and feet. Hind feet have five pads
on the sole (six in *Microtus*). Fur is short, dense and soft; dark
brown on back, lighter on sides, grey below. Tail is 30–35 per
cent of head and body. Hind foot less than 15 mm (0.6 ins).
Range Broken distribution in deciduous woodland and steppe
zones from France through central Europe to the Ukraine and
River Don.

Habitat Grassland and open woodland to over 2,000 m
(6,500 ft).
Behaviour Generally rather subterranean, living in an
extensive tunnel system just below soil surface. Mainly
nocturnal.
Breeding Up to nine litters of two or three young per year.
Food Rhizomes, bulbs and roots.
Similar species Related species are only separated by small
differences in the skull or by chromosomes:
ALPINE PINE VOLE *P. multiplex* in Switzerland, Austria, Italy
and France to 200 m (650 ft);
TATRA PINE VOLE *P. tatricus* at 1,500–2,300 m (4,800–7,500
ft) in spruce forests of Tatra Mountains;
BAVARIAN PINE VOLE *P. bavaricus* from one valley in the
Bavarian Alps (perhaps now extinct);
LIECHTENSTEIN'S PINE VOLE *P. liechtensteini* from north-
western former Yugoslavia;
plus another species, *P. dinniki*, from Macedonia and Greece.

Lusitanian Pine Vole
Pitymys lusitanicus

Size head & body 85–105 mm (3.25–4 ins);
tail 20–30 mm (0.75–1.25 ins)
Weight 15–23 g (0.5–1 oz)

Identification Almost inseparable in the field from the *P. subterraneus* (European pine vole) complex. Can be more yellowish above, paler silver-grey below and the tail is very short. The hind foot is very large (15–18 mm, 0.6–0.75 ins). The main differences are fine details of the teeth.
Range North-western half of Iberia and extreme south-west of France.

Habitat Open woodland.
Behaviour Mainly crepuscular and nocturnal. Digs burrows with entrances marked by spoil heaps.
Breeding One litter of one to five young.
Food Plant material.
Similar species The Lusitanian pine vole is another example of a small group of species separated by small differences in the skull or by chromosome characteristics:
MEDITERRANEAN PINE VOLE *P. duodecimcostatus* in south-eastern France (Provence and the Rhône Valley) and in eastern and southern Spain;
THOMAS'S PINE VOLE *P. thomasi* in southern coastal areas of former Yugoslavia, in Greece and perhaps Albania.

Savi's Pine Vole
Pitymys savii

Size head & body 75–105 mm (3–4 ins);
tail 20–35 mm (0.75–1.25 ins)
Weight 10–25 g (0.5–1 oz)

Identification Similar to European pine vole, but paler and
greyer, with hind foot a little longer and differences in
dentition. Savi's pine vole is one of a complex of three closely
related species.
Range Italy and Sicily. The various species of this group of
pine voles do not overlap in distribution with other pine voles.
Thus they occur at lower altitudes where the range overlaps
with the European pine vole and its allies, and at higher
altitudes where the range overlaps with the Lusitanian pine
vole and its allies.
Habitat Forest, grassland, gardens.
Behaviour Mainly crepuscular and nocturnal. Nests of
grass in underground burrows.
Breeding Two to four young.
Food Plant material.
Similar species *P. gerbii* in south-western France, the
Pyrenees and north-western Spain;
P. felteni in southern former Yugoslavia (Serbia).

Snow Vole
Microtus nivalis

Size head & body 100–140 mm (4–5.5 ins);
tail 50–75 mm (2–3 ins)
Weight 30–65 g (1.25–2.5 oz)

Identification Very pale grey-brown with relatively long
tail (50 per cent of head and body length). Has especially
prominent whiskers and relatively long ears compared with
Martino's snow vole.
Range Scattered distribution in Iberian mountains, the
Pyrenees, Alps, Apennines, Balkans, Tatra and Carpathian
mountains. Also lowlands of southern France in Gard.
Habitat Open grassy slopes of mountains above the treeline
to 4,000 m (13,000 ft), among scree and scrub. In lowlands
of France it is found in low, dry wooded hills.
Behaviour Diurnal and gregarious, sometimes basks in
sunshine. Behaviour similar to root vole, but it does not dig
burrows, preferring to make a network of runs under rocks.
Climbs around rock scree and jumps from rock to rock.
Breeding Similar to other grass voles, but breeding season
is shorter with one or two litters of two to seven young born
between May and August.
Food Alpine herbs and grasses, low shrubs and berries.
Similar species Martino's Snow Vole
Dinaromys bogdanovi (see page 146).

Field Vole
Microtus agrestis

Size head & body 90–135 mm (3.5–5.25 ins);
      tail 25–45 mm (1–1.75 ins)
Weight 15–50 g (0.5–2 oz)

Identification Back greyish to yellowish brown, usually
shaggy, the underside grey occasionally tinged with buff. The
ears are well haired, including inside at the base. The tail is
distinctly darker above and about 30 per cent of head and
body length.
Range Throughout British mainland and on many Hebridean
islands, but absent from Ireland and many major islands.
From the Atlantic seaboard through Europe from northern
Scandinavia and Finland to the Pyrenees and eastwards north
of the Alps and Balkan mountains. An isolated population in
northern Spain and Portugal (*M. rozianus*).
Habitat A montane species in the south, but elsewhere in
rough grassland, also in woodland, hedges, dunes, scree
and moorland.
Behaviour More or less nocturnal. Makes a network of
runways in dense grass, often marked with green faeces and
pieces of cut grass.
Breeding Breed from four weeks old and, with a gestation
period of twenty days and lactation period of two to three
weeks, can build up high densities in some years.
Food Grasses, rushes, sedges and green leaves plus bark,
roots and rhizomes; seasonally, carrion and insects.
Similar species Common Vole *M. arvalis* (see page 154).

Common Vole
Microtus arvalis

Size head & body 90–134 mm (3.5–5.25 ins);
tail 27–45 mm (1–1.75 ins)
Weight 20–67 g (0.75–2.5 oz)

Identification Closely resembles field vole, but the fur is
shorter and the ears are less hairy, with the inside being
almost naked. The tail is a little darker above than below
and is about 30 per cent of the head and body length.
Range Eastwards from Denmark and Baltic coast south to
northern Spain. Absent from most of southern France and
Mediterranean peninsulas. Also on islands such as Yeu
(France), Spitzbergen, Orkney and Channel islands (these
are perhaps introductions).

Habitat Short grassland mainly, but also coniferous and
deciduous plantations, marshes and moors, meadows,
ditches and gardens.
Behaviour Active day and night in two to three-hour cycle
of resting and foraging. Makes conspicuous runways and
burrows.
Breeding Starting in February, many litters of three to six
young can be produced each year. Marked population cycles.
Food Leaves, stems and roots of a wide range of grasses and
herbaceous plants.
Conservation Regarded as a pest in arable land during
periods of population increase.
Similar species *M. epiroticus* (or *subarvalis*) is inseparable in
the field and widely overlaps in its range from eastern Finland
and European Russia to southern former Yugoslavia, Bulgaria
and, as *M. rossiaemeridionalis*, in Greece.

Root Vole
Microtus oeconomus

Size head & body 90–150 mm (3.5–6 ins);
    tail 30–65 mm (1.25–2.5 ins)
Weight 35–50 g (1.25–2 oz)

Identification Slightly larger than field vole with relatively
longer tail (about 40 per cent of head and body length), brown
upper fur distinctly darker than silvery grey belly.
Range Tundra and taiga zone, from scattered populations in
Scandinavia and Finland eastwards. South of the Baltic it is
found from northern Germany east to northern Romania and
through the Ukraine. Isolated populations in the Netherlands
and Hungary.
Habitat Grassland but often in wetter areas than some other
grass voles, including swamp, moist meadow and damp forest.
Behaviour Mainly nocturnal. Tunnels extensively, but makes
grass nests above ground.
Breeding Similar to that of field vole. Populations fluctuate
in Scandinavia, where three or four litters of four to seven
young can be produced in a year.
Food Green part of plants, principally grasses, and roots.
Conservation Netherlands population is very vulnerable.
Similar species Other grass voles (*Microtus* species, see
pages 152–156).

Gunther's Vole
Microtus guentheri

Size head & body 100–120 mm (4–4.75 ins);
tail 20–35 mm (0.75–1.25 ins)
Weight 35–70 g (1.25–2.75 oz)

Identification A typical grass vole with eyes and ears smaller
than in species of red-backed voles (*Clethrionomys* species)
and larger than in the pine voles (*Pitymys* species). Has a
shorter tail (about 25 per cent of head and body length) than
the common vole, is of a paler colour and has white feet.
Range From southern former Yugoslavia, Bulgaria and Greece
south through Asia Minor to
Israel and Libya.

Habitat Dry grassland, pasture, arable field and irrigated
grasslands.
Behaviour Similar to common vole, and uses subsurface
burrows, enabling it to occupy cultivated ground.
Breeding Litters usually of five to six young, but up to
seventeen has been recorded, and populations fluctuate.
Food Grasses and roots.
Conservation Sometimes an agricultural pest.
Similar species Other grass voles (*Microtus* species, see
pages 152–155), but distribution does not overlap.
CABRERA'S VOLE *Microtus cabrerae* is a large grass vole of
central and south-eastern Spain and Portugal north to the
French Pyrenees. It has a very short tail and particularly
long and dark guard hairs on the rump.

Harvest Mouse
Micromys minutus

Size head & body 50–80 mm (2–3 ins);
tail: 50–75 mm (2–3 ins)
Weight 5–11 g (0.25–0.5 oz)

Identification The smallest European rodent. It is slender
with a short blunt muzzle, short hairy ears, slender feet with a
greater toe-spread than usual in mice. The slender, sparsely-
haired tail has a very prehensile tip. Russet-orange upper fur,
white below.
Range Throughout central Europe north to the Baltic coast
and Finland, south to the Mediterranean coast (but more or
less absent from the Mediterranean peninsulas). Found in
southern England north to mid-Yorkshire in the east with
isolated populations in coastal Wales and southern Scotland.
Absent from Ireland.
Habitat Tall, dense vegetation in hedgerow, road and ditch
banks, reed beds and rushes, bramble thickets, cereals and
sometimes other crops. Salt marshes and wet meadows are
vacated during winter flooding.
Behaviour Very agile climber, active mostly at dusk and
dawn. It does not hibernate. Builds nests of woven grass stems.
Breeding From May to October or later and can produce
three or four litters of about five young in a year.
Food Mainly seeds, fruit
and berries as well as
relatively large insects.
Leaves and buds are also
eaten and sometimes
fungi, moss, roots and
other invertebrates.
Conservation Intensive
land management has
caused declines.

Yellow-necked Mouse
Apodemus flavicollis

Size head & body 95–125 mm (3.75–5 ins);
   tail 80–130 mm (3–5 ins);
Weight 20–55 g (0.75–2 oz)

Identification Slightly larger than the wood mouse, with more orange brown above and paler below. In the north, the yellow chest spot is always present as a complete transverse collar; in the south and east, the chest mark is not so distinctive. Tail usually longer than length of head and body.

Range Extends further north than the wood mouse into Scandinavia and Finland to about 64°N, but is more restricted and montane towards southern Europe, being absent from much of the Low Countries, France, Iberia and lowland Italy. Patchy distribution in southern Britain.

Habitat Mature deciduous, preferably moist, woodland; alpine coniferous woodland; hedgerows, orchards and rural gardens. Less frequent than wood mouse in scrub and open habitats and more often enters buildings in winter.

Behaviour More or less solitary; not as aggressive as the wood mouse. Can be markedly arboreal, but also uses extensive burrow systems. Nests of leaves are made in similar situations to those of the wood mouse.

Breeding Normally two or three litters of five to six young are born in a year.

Food Similar to the wood mouse, perhaps with a greater concentration on seeds. This species also makes considerable caches of food.

Similar species Separation from the Wood Mouse *A. sylvaticus* is very difficult in parts of range.

Wood Mouse
Apodemus sylvaticus

Size head & body: 80–110 mm (3–4.25 ins);
    tail 70–115 mm (2.75–4.5 ins)
Weight 13-39 g (0.5–1.75 oz)

Identification Typical mouse with a pointed muzzle, large dark protruding eyes, large, bare ears and a long tail. Upper fur dark brown with some yellow, particularly on the flanks; underside very pale. Tail darker above than below, sparsely haired and as long as head and body.
Range The most common and widespread mouse in Europe north to the Baltic states and southern Scandinavia (and Iceland), south to include western North Africa and most Mediterranean islands. Found throughout the British Isles and on most islands.

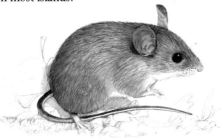

Habitat Deciduous woodland and steppes, hedgerows, grassland, arable land, heaths, bogs, dunes and gardens well into urban areas.
Behaviour Mainly nocturnal and solitary. Very agile. Usually nests below ground, often under the roots of woody plants. Sometimes, especially in autumn and winter, nests in tree-holes, nest boxes or buildings.
Breeding Litters of four to seven young can be produced at about monthly intervals between March and October.
Food A wide range of food: seeds, fruit, green matter, buds and seedlings in spring. Food is often cached in burrows (especially nuts). Food remains left at regular feeding sites, such as in disused birds' nests. Invertebrates, including insect larvae, centipedes, snails and earthworms, are important and even a frog is recorded.
Similar species Yellow-necked Mouse *A. flavicollis*.

Pygmy Field Mouse
Apodemus microps

Size head & body 70–95 mm (2.75–3.75 ins);
tail 65–95 mm (2.5–3.75 ins)
Weight 13–27 g (0.5–1 oz)

Identification Smaller than the wood mouse with a greyer coat. Chest spot present or absent. Feet larger (17–20 mm, around 0.75 ins) than similarly coloured pale forms of the house mouse.
Range Lowland eastern Europe, principally the Czech Republic, Slovakia and Romania, but also in adjacent Poland, Austria, Hungary, former Yugoslavia and Bulgaria as well as Asia Minor.
Habitat Relatively dry open areas of long grass, scrub and crops.
Behaviour Little is recorded.
Breeding Litters of three to eight born from March to August.
Food Seeds, weeds, grasses and corn, although about one tenth of its diet is invertebrates such as earthworms and insect larvae.
Similar species Another similar species has recently been described: the ALPINE WOOD MOUSE *A. alpicola* from the European Alps.

Broad-toothed or Rock Mouse
Apodemus mystacinus

Size head & body 100–130 mm (4–5 ins),
    tail 105–140 mm (4–5.5 ins)
Weight 30-60 g (1.25–2.5 oz)

Identification A large species with large ears, 17–21 mm
(around 0.75 ins), and the hind foot measures 24–28 mm
(over 1 ins). It is greyish without a chest spot and so might be
confused with the larger ship rat. Distinctly long whiskers.
Range South-eastern Europe in former Yugoslavia, Albania,
southern Bulgaria and northern Greece; also along the
Adriatic coast and on inshore islands south to Crete. To the
east it is found in Asia Minor, Palestine and adjacent parts of
Iraq and Georgia.
Habitat Dry woodland and rocky scrubby hillsides.
Behaviour Little is recorded.
Breeding One to three litters of four to six young.
Food Seeds and other plant material, some insects.

Striped Field Mouse
Apodemus agrarius

Size head & body 90–115 mm (3.5–4.5 ins);
tail 70–90 mm (2.75–3.5 ins)
Weight 15–30 g (0.5–1 oz)

Identification Distinctive bold dark stripe along the yellow-brown back from the crown to the rump. Tail is shorter than the head and body. Birch mice also have a distinct dorsal stripe, but have a tail much longer than the body.

Range Fragmented in north-western Germany, southern Denmark and Finland. From other parts of northern Germany and from northern Italy through much of eastern Europe, south to northern Greece and east to Lake Baikal.

Habitat Lowland to about 800 m (2,600 ft) scrub, hedgerows and woodland edges, often quite moist. Crop fields, haystacks and barns.

Behaviour Less nocturnal and less arboreal and saltatorial (likely to jump) than other members of genus. Digs burrows with nest chambers and storage areas.

Breeding Between April and October produces several litters of five to seven young per year. Populations can fluctuate widely, sometimes resulting in it becoming a crop pest.

Food Eats green plant material and often caches seeds. Probably takes a higher proportion of animal matter than the wood mouse – insects and their larvae, worms, molluscs and small vertebrates, the latter probably mainly eaten as carrion.

Similar species Birch mice (*Sicista* species, see pages 170–171).

Ship Rat
Rattus rattus

Size head & body 140–240 mm (5.5–9.5 ins);
tail 140–260 mm (5.5–10 ins)
Weight 150–250 g (5–9 oz)

Identification Compared with the common rat, the ship rat has a 'cleaner' and more slender appearance with a more pointed muzzle, larger eyes, larger ears 24–27 mm (over 1 ins) long, which are thinner and almost hairless, and a scaly tail that is at least as long as the head and body. Fur colour varies greatly.
Range Originating from the south-eastern Asian tropics, it is now found throughout the Mediterranean region and North Africa. It occurs sporadically further north to the Baltic region and establishes temporary populations in ports. In the British Isles, the only recent records are from London, Avonmouth and Cork, although there are 'wild' colonies on some islands.
Habitat Mainly urban, but does reach small villages and isolated farms in cultivated areas in southern Europe.
Behaviour Mainly nocturnal, especially in human habitation. It lives in groups with a dominant male. The nests are usually above ground, often in the rafters of buildings.
Breeding Three to five litters of six to seven young can be produced in a year.
Food Principally plant matter but also eats some animal matter. Agricultural crops, particularly fruit and cereals.
Conservation Widely regarded as a pest.

Common Rat
Rattus norvegicus

Size head & body 150–300 mm (6–12 ins);
tail 140– 230 mm (5.5–9 ins)
Weight 150–500 g (5–17.5 oz)

Identification Larger than the ship rat with a somewhat
blunter muzzle. Eyes smaller, as are the finely furred ears, at
19–22 mm (less than 1 ins) long. Tail relatively shorter and
thicker. Fur shaggier and greasy.
Range Originating probably from the eastern CIS or China,
now world-wide. Widely distributed in Europe, including many
islands, but less common in southern Europe. Throughout
Britain, except exposed mountain regions and many smaller
off-shore islands.

Habitat Principally urban, but also occurs in cultivated land,
coasts and estuaries. Mainly disturbed habitats including farms,
refuse, sewers, urban waterways, cellars and warehouses.
Behaviour Mainly nocturnal. Colonial. Climbs well in
buildings, but is not as fast and agile as the ship rat. Swims
readily and well. Burrows into banks or under rocks and
logs. Usually nests below ground.
Breeding Up to five litters of six to eight (even twelve)
young produced in a year.
Food More omnivorous than the ship rat: cereals, root crops,
brassicas, weed seeds and some invertebrates such as
earthworms. In towns this is supplemented with meat, fish
and bones. The seashore diet includes *Spartina* grass and
crustaceans. A great range of other items is recorded. Small
food-caches are made in burrows.
Conservation Widely regarded as a pest.

Western House Mouse
Mus domesticus

Size head & body 70–100 mm (3–4 ins);
tail 65–90 mm (2.5–3.5 ins)
Weight 10–20 g (0.35–0.75 oz)

Identification Fur is dull grey-brown above and slightly
lighter below, and never with the chest spot seen in some
wood mice. The tail is about as long as the head and body.
Ears, eyes and feet are smaller than those of wood mice.
Range Throughout Britain and Ireland close to habitation;
in mainland Europe from the west of Denmark across to the
northern end of the Adriatic Sea and the southern Balkans.

Habitat Mainly an indoor species, but survives well in the
open in the absence of major competition, such as on islands.
Its adaptability to human habitation is extreme: from central
heating ducts to refrigerated stores and miles down coal mines.
Behaviour Mainly nocturnal. It climbs, jumps and swims well
and often makes burrows. Nests of any available material can
be simple platforms in a chamber or may be enclosed spheres.
Breeding Litters of five to eight young can be produced at
monthly intervals throughout the year when indoors or in the
summer when out of doors.
Food Variable, but principally cereal seeds, although insects
are significant in populations away from habitation.
Similar species EASTERN HOUSE MOUSE *Mus musculus* , a
little larger with a longer tail and other differences too slight
for reliable field recognition, is distributed east of *M. domesticus*
with a narrow band of hybridization in Jutland (Denmark).
M. poschiavinus, an indoor species of southern Switzerland
and adjacent parts of the Italian Alps, is only separable on
details of chromosomes.

Algerian Mouse
Mus spretus

Size head & body 70–85 mm (3–3.5 ins);
tail 55–70 mm (2.25–2.75 ins)
Weight 10–15 g (0.25–0.5 oz)

Identification Upper fur is distinctly more yellow-brown than grey, and well demarcated from the white or pale grey underside. Tail relatively short and distinctly bicoloured. Feet are white.
Range Extreme southern France south to Iberia and the Balearic Islands. Also North Africa from Morocco to Tunisia and in isolated coastal areas further east.
Habitat Cultivated land and gardens, often associated with habitation as well as occurring in scrub and open woodland. Said to generally prefer moister habitats.
Behaviour Relatively little studied. What is known suggests that is more solitary than other mice.
Breeding Five to ten litters of up to nine young.
Food Omnivorous.
Similar species STEPPE MOUSE *Mus spicilegus* is larger, but with the same colouration, and occurs in the steppe zones of south-eastern Europe east from Austria. More or less colonial and builds distinctive storage mounds containing up to 10 kg (22 lb) of grain, accessed via extensive burrow systems.
M. abbotti, from former Yugoslavia to Asia Minor and northern Iran, is larger and has only a slight notch in the upper incisors, instead of the distinct notch seen in these other species.

Spiny Mouse
Acomys cahirinus

Size head & body 90–120 mm (3.5–4.75 ins);
   tail 90–120 mm (3.5–4.75 ins)
Weight 40– 85 g (1.5–3 oz)

Identification Distinguished from the wood mouse by the many very stiff bristles on the back from the neck to the rump. The ears are very large and usually have a pale patch behind them. The fur on the back is a yellowish brown, sometimes rather grey, and the underside is white with a clear line of demarcation from the upper fur. The tail is rather thick and scaly, but is easily and often broken.
Range Southern edge of the Sahara and south to much of East Africa. It also occurs in Egypt and Arabia north to southern Asia Minor and on the island of Crete (where it might be a separate species, *A. minous*, or an introduction).
Habitat Readily enters houses, especially in the winter, but also lives in dry scrub on rocky hillsides.
Behaviour Active at any time of day or night and builds a rudimentary nest.
Breeding Generally has small litters of two to three, but the young are born relatively well-developed.
Food Mainly seeds and other plant material, though insects and snails are also eaten.

Greater Mole-Rat
Spalax microphthalmus

Size head & body: 200–300 mm (8–12 ins)
Weight 220–520 g (8 oz–1 lb)

Identification Looks like a short, fat, hairy sausage, with
large flattened head and no apparent neck. No outer ears or
tail, and the eyes are completely covered with skin. Small
limbs but powerful front teeth. The soft velvety fur is usually
greyish tinged with yellow above. Row of stiff almost white
hairs from nose to ear opening. Hind foot is more than
25 mm (1 ins) long.
Range From the River Volga and the plains north of the
central Caucasus west into Romania, Bulgaria and
northern Greece.

Habitat Dry fertile steppes, occasionally in open forest edges
or cultivated fields.
Behaviour Almost exclusively subterranean, active mainly
in the evening and at night. Each animal has its own extensive
tunnel system. The excavated soil is piled above the nests in
mounds that may reach 2 m (6.5 ft) in height. They do not
hibernate.
Breeding A single litter of four to five young born in the
spring.
Food Roots, bulbs and rhizomes taken from below ground,
with sometimes grass, seeds and a few insects. Large supplies
of food may be stored
Similar species European population may be a separate
species: *S. graecus.*

Lesser Mole-Rat
Nannospalax leucodon

Size head & body 150–260 mm (6–10.25 ins)
Weight 140-220 g (5–8 oz)

Identification Slightly smaller and browner than the greater mole-rat, although colour varies. The length of the hind foot is usually less than 25 mm (under 1 ins), and the row of stiff hairs on the face is not distinguished in colour.
Range Found from the Danube delta west to Hungary, north to the Czech Republic, Slovakia (and formerly south Poland) and south to Yugoslavia and Greece. To the east it occurs through the southern Ukraine, Caucasus and Asia Minor to Syria and Israel and in coastal Egypt and Libya.

Habitat Burrow systems in steppes.
Breeding Usually a single litter born in the spring.
Food Similar to the greater mole-rat.
Similar species On the basis of chromosomal studies, a further seven species have been recognized from various parts of former Yugoslavia, Bulgaria and Greece. The status of these, and some forms where morphological differences have been suggested, is still under discussion. Even the generic classification is unsettled. Some authorities would argue for the recognition of only three species in one genus, while others argue for a variable large number of species in several genera.

Northern Birch Mouse
Sicista betulina
Rodentia; Zapodidae

Size head & body 50–70 mm (2–2.75 ins);
   tail 80–105 mm (3.25–4 ins)
Weight 6.5–13 g (0.25–0.5 oz)

Identification A very long prehensile tail and a black line on
the back immediately distinguish birch mice. In this species,
the back is a uniform greyish yellow to reddish ochre apart
from the black stripe, which runs from the head to the base
of the tail. The tail is about one and a half times the length
of the head and body.
Range Patchy distribution in the boreal and montane forest
zones from Scandinavia (including Denmark), Finland
and the Carpathian mountains, through western Russia to
Lake Baikal.
Habitat In the north, it lives in woodland, especially damp
birch and spruce with dense undergrowth; more montane in
the south.
Behaviour Distinctive bounding movement on the ground,
but climbs with agility. Nocturnal. Nests in burrows, under
bark or in old logs. The nest often has a lower chamber acting
as a food store. Hibernates between October and April in a
mossy nest underground or in a rotten tree stump.
Breeding One litter of two to six young each year.
Food Mainly adult and larval insects and other invertebrates.
Some plant material (buds, seeds, fruit, berries and nuts) is
eaten, especially in the autumn.
Conservation Generally scarce and threatened.

Southern Birch Mouse
Sicista subtilis

Size head & body 55–70 mm (2.25–2.75 ins);
tail 70–85 mm (2.75–3.25 ins)
Weight 9.5–14 g (0.25–0.5 oz)

Identification The tail of this species not as long as that of its
northern counterpart, about 1.3 times the length of the head
and body. It also differs in having the dark central stripe of the
back bordered by pale stripes. Stripe often fails to reach head.
Range Steppes of eastern Austria, the Czech
Republic, Slovakia,
Hungary and Romania
through southern
Russia east to
Lake
Baikal.

Habitat Prefers more open country to its northern relative,
living mostly at low altitude in rough grassland, scrub, open
woodland and the margins of cultivation.
Behaviour Life style is similar to that of the northern birch
mouse. May hibernate for short periods.
Breeding A low reproduction rate, like the northern birch
mouse: one litter of two to eight young born in May/June.
Food Largely on insects and other invertebrates
supplemented with plant material.
Similar species The Striped Field Mouse *A. agrarius* (see
page 162) also has a distinct black dorsal stripe and lives in
the same areas, but its tail is much shorter.

Fat Dormouse
Glis glis
Rodentia; Gliridae

Size head & body 135–190 mm (5.25–7.5 ins);
tail 100–150 mm (4–6 ins)
Weight 50–200 g (2–7 oz)

Identification Twice the size of the hazel dormouse. Grey-
brown above, almost bluish grey when freshly moulted, paler
on the flanks and white below. The tail is very bushy and
flattened dorso-ventrally. There is a darker patch around the
large black eye, and vaguely darker patches at the base of the
whiskers and on the outside of the legs.
Range Widespread in the wooded parts of Europe from the
Mediterranean to close to the Baltic Sea, but absent from most
of Iberia, northern France, the Low Countries and Denmark.
On most major Mediterranean islands except Balearics.
Introduced to England around Tring.
Habitat Mature mixed and deciduous woodland, orchards
and gardens.
Behaviour Nocturnal. Lives in groups. An able climber,
spending most of its life in the tree canopy and readily entering
roofs. Rests in a tree-hole or nest of leaves, and hibernates in
tree-holes, in the thatch or roof space of buildings, or burrows
among tree roots.
Breeding A single litter of four to six young (but between one
and eleven recorded).
Food Fruit, nuts, buds, bark
(especially fruit trees
and willow) and
some fungi, but also
insects, snails,
carrion and
occasionally
birds' eggs or
nestlings.
Sometimes
stores
food.

Hazel Dormouse
Muscardinus avellanarius

Size head & body 60–90 mm (2.5–3.5 ins);
tail 5.5–75 mm; (2.25–3 ins)
Weight 15–25 g (0.5–1 oz)

Identification Has a thickly furred but not bushy tail. The fur
is soft and dense, bright orange-brown or golden colour above,
pale buff below with white on the throat.
Range Widespread in Europe from the Baltic Sea to the
Mediterranean. Absent from Iberia and Denmark. Isolated
populations in southern Sweden, Britain, Sicily, Corfu and
Asia Minor. Widespread in Britain, but is local south from
mid-Wales, Leicestershire and Suffolk, also isolated
populations as far north as southern Scotland.
Habitat Deciduous woodland
with a dense shrub layer,
particularly coppiced
woodland. Sometimes
in good
hedgerows.

Behaviour Nocturnal. An agile climber, spending most of its
time above ground. Sometimes communal, especially in
hibernation. Nests, with no marked entrance hole, of finely
stripped bark (plus some grass, leaves and moss) are made
up to 10 m (33 ft) above ground in dense vegetation,
tree-holes or bird and bat boxes. Hibernation is in nests
usually at or below ground level and in boxes.
Breeding One or two litters of about four young are born
between May and September.
Food Hazel, sweet chestnut, ash and beech seeds. Also
flowers, berries, buds, shoots and bark, many insects and
occasionally nestling birds.
Conservation Threatened in parts of range.

Garden Dormouse
Eliomys quercinus

Size head & body 100–170 mm (4–6.75 ins);
      tail 90–120 mm (3.5–4.75 ins)
Weight 65–100 g (2.5–4 oz)

Identification Grey-brown on back with a slightly red tinge
and a yellow-white underside. A black mask from around the
eye runs past the base of the ear to the neck. A white spot lies
in front of the ear, which is large and almost naked. The tail is
more or less white below; dark brown above basally, black
towards the tip with a terminal brush of white-tipped hairs.
Range Widespread in central and southern Europe, and
through the wooded parts of European Russia to Finland,
but absent from most of the Baltic coast, Low Countries
and large parts of south-eastern Europe. Isolated populations
on Dalmatian coast, Sicily and most Mediterranean islands
to the west.

Habitat Deciduous and coniferous woodland, gardens and
orchards; readily enters houses in the autumn. Also in scrub
and rocky terrain.
Behaviour More or less nocturnal. An agile climber and nests
in tree holes, clefts in walls or among rocks and in old birds'
nests. Hibernates.
Breeding A litter of four to five young is born in May or June.
Food Fruit and nuts plus a variety of other vegetable matter.
It probably eats more animal matter than other dormice,
including insects, snails, eggs and baby mice.

Forest Dormouse
Dryomys nitedula

Size head & body 80–130 mm (3.25–5.25 ins);
tail 80–95 mm (3.25–3.75 ins)
Weight 16–30 g (0.5–1 oz)

Identification The fur above is a light grey to a warm
yellowish or reddish brown, and the underside is a rather
dirty yellowish white. The black mask only extends to the
base of the ear. The short ears, 12–15 mm (0.5–0.6 ins), only
just project beyond the fur, and are well furred. The tail is
uniformly bushy, but not as bushy as the fat dormouse.

Range South-eastern Poland west to Alps and south through
the Balkans, with isolated populations in southern Italy.
Habitat Mainly deciduous woodland, especially with a thick
shrub layer, but sometimes in coniferous forests (Carpathians).
Behaviour Summer nest is a sphere of grass or twigs in the
tree canopy, in tree-holes, nest boxes, abandoned bird's nests
or underground burrows. It hibernates in the north of its
range in a burrow or among tree roots. Nocturnal and an
agile climber.
Breeding A single litter of two to six young.
Food Seeds, fruits and green plant material makes up the
bulk of the food, but some insects and eggs and nestling birds
are also eaten.
Similar species Similar to the larger Garden Dormouse
Eliomys quercinus.

Mouse-tailed Dormouse
Myomimus bulgaricus

Size head & body 70–110 mm (2.75–4.25 ins);
    tail 60–80 mm (2.5–3.25 ins)
Weight 16–30 g (0.5–1 oz)

Identification Pale grey above, white below. The feet and
claws are also white. The tail is a little shorter than the head
and body with uniformly short hairs. It is probably more
terrestrial than other dormice, and so might be confused with
some mice and voles. The combination of grey fur, long tail
and short round ears separate it from all except the Balkan
vole which is a little larger and has smaller eyes.
Range South-eastern Bulgaria and western Turkey.
Habitat Dry scrub and woodland.
Breeding Little is known.
Food Mainly seeds.
Conservation Little is known.
Similar species While the living representatives of this
group seem to have caused confusion and dissent among
taxonomists, their problems have only been exacerbated by
available sub-fossil remains. Sometimes the name *M. roachi*
has been used in the belief that this is the same species as one
described from sub-fossil material from Israel, but different
from the population extant in south-western Turkmenistan
and northern Iran (which is called *M. personatus*).

Crested Porcupine
Hystrix cristata
Rodentia; Hystricidae

Size head & body 500–700 mm (20–27.5 ins);
    tail 50–120 mm (2–5 ins)
Weight 10–17 kg (22–37.5 lb)

Identification A large and unmistakable animal with its
unique array of spines.
Range Sicily, southern Italy and previously southern former
Yugoslavia, Albania and northern Greece. It may still survive
in northern former Yugoslavia, but nowhere is its status well
known. Probably all European populations are introductions.
Many recent escapes from zoological collections have occurred.
Has survived in the wild for up to two years in Britain.
Habitat Open arid woodland and scrub.
Behaviour Nocturnal and may become inactive for a few
days during cold winter weather. Lives in small groups and
lays up in large deep burrows or caves. The quills are used
by the animal reversing into an enemy, using its great bulk
to help lodge the spines. Usually before that it will growl and
jump as part of its threat. If it feels seriously threatened itself,
it can roll up.
Breeding A single litter of two to four young in an
underground den in summer.
Food Mainly roots, bulbs and bark. It also takes green plant
material and occasionally scavenges.
Conservation In need of strict protection.
Similar species HIMALAYAN PORCUPINE *H. brachyura* has
survived in the wild in Britain.

Coypu
Myocaster coypu
Rodentia; Myocastoridae

Size head & body 500–650 mm (20–26 ins);
tail 300–450 mm (12–18 ins)
Weight 5–7.5 kg (11–16.5 lb)

Identification A very large rodent with bright orange teeth
and a tapering cylindrical rat-like tail. Glossy dark brown
upper fur is overlain with dense yellow-brown guard hairs.
Hind feet webbed, ears small.

Range Introduced from South America for its fur; established
in England (East Anglia, where it is now probably extinct),
the Netherlands, Belgium, France, Germany and Italy.
In some areas, such as Poland, escapees seem unable to
survive the harsh winters.

Habitat Extensive reed beds, fens and other freshwater
marshland. Occasionally in brackish
coastal marshes.

Behaviour Mainly
nocturnal, but
more diurnal in
winter. Aquatic,
with an awkward
walking gait and
bounding gallop
on land. A
complex burrow
system in banks has
entrances at water
level or above. Sometimes
builds large nests in reeds. Often well-defined runs lead to
the water's edge and contain the unique droppings, slug-like
with longitudinal ribbing.

Breeding Generally aseasonal, with only about two litters of
three to eight young a year.

Food Aquatic vegetation: roots and rhizomes; shoots and
stems or leaf bases; and fruits, including the seeds of water lily.
Also occasionally eats freshwater mussels, grass near the
water's edge and sometimes crops.

Conservation Damage to waterway banks, crops and
indigenous flora encourages eradication campaigns.

Index

Hamster, Romanian 140
Hare, Arctic 128
Hare, Brown 129
Hare, Mountain 128
Hedgehog, Algerian 13
Hedgehog, Long-Eared 13
Hedgehog, Vagrant 13
Hedgehog, Western 12
Horse, Domestic 111

Ibex, Alpine 125
Ibex, Spanish 125

Jackal, Northern 63

Lemming, Arctic 142
Lemming, Norway 142
Lemming, Wood 141
Lynx, Eurasian 85

Marmot, Alpine 133
Marmot, Steppe 133
Marten, Beech 78
Marten, Pine 77
Mink, American 72
Mink, European 72
Mole, Balkan 29
Mole, European 27
Mole, Mediterranean 28
Mole, Roman 29
Mole-Rat, Greater 168
Mole-Rat, Lesser 169
Mongoose, Egyptian 83
Mouflon 126
Mouse, Algerian 166
Mouse, Birch, Northern 170
Mouse, Birch, Southern 171
Mouse, Broad-Toothed 161
Mouse, Field, Pygmy 160
Mouse, Field, Striped 162
Mouse, Harvest 157
Mouse, House, Eastern 165
Mouse, House, Western 165
Mouse, Rock 161
Mouse, Spiny 167

Mouse, Steppe 166
Mouse, Wood 159
Mouse, Yellow-Necked 158
Muntjac, Reeve's 114
Muskrat 148

Narwhal 104

Orca 96
Otter, European 81
Ox, Musk 121

Pig, Guinea 138
Pipistrelle, Kuhl's 48
Pipistrelle, Nathusius's 47
Pipistrelle, Savi's 49
Polecat, Marbled 76
Polecat, Steppe 75
Polecat, Western 74
Porcupine, Crested 177
Porcupine, Himalayan 177
Porpoise, Common 94
Porpoise, Harbour 94

Rabbit, European 127
Raccoon, Common 67
Rat, Common 164
Rat, Ship 163
Reindeer 119
Rorqual, Common 108

Seal, Bearded 91
Seal, Grey 90
Seal, Harbour 87
Seal, Harp 89
Seal, Hooded 93
Seal, Monk, Mediterranean 92
Seal, Ringed 88
Shrew, Alpine 19
Shrew, Common, Eurasian 17
Shrew, Dusky 18
Shrew, Laxmann's 16
Shrew, Least 14
Shrew, Pygmy, Eurasian 15
Shrew, Siberian 14

Index of Latin Names

Lepus capensis 129
Lepus timidus 128
Lutra lutra 81
Lynx lynx 85

Macaca sylvanus 61
Macropus rufogriseus 11
Marmota marmota 133
Marmotabobak 133
Martes foina 78
Martes martes 77
Megaptera novaeangliae 110
Meles meles 80
Mesocricetus auratus 140
Mesocricetus newtoni 140
Mesoplodon bidens 107
Mesoplodon densirostris 107
Mesoplodon europaeus 107
Mesoplodon grayi 107
Mesoplodon mirus 107
Micromys minutus 157
Microtus agrestis 153
Microtus arvalis 154
Microtus cabrerae 156
Microtus guentheri 156
Microtus nivalis 152
Microtus oeconomus 155
Miniopterus schreibersii 59
Monachus monachus 92
Monodon monoceros 104
Muntiacus reevesi 114
Mus domesticus 165
Mus musculus 165
Mus spicilegus 166
Mus spretus 166
Muscardinus avellanarius 173
Mustela erminea 70
Mustela eversmanni 75
Mustela furo 73
Mustela lutreola 72
Mustela nivalis 71
Mustela putorius 74
Mustela vison 72
Myocaster coypu 178
Myomimus bulgaricus 176

Myopus schisticolor 141
Myotis bechsteinii 40
Myotis blythii 42
Myotis brandtii 37
Myotis capaccinii 44
Myotis dasycneme 45
Myotis daubentonii 43
Myotis emarginatus 38
Myotis lucifugus, 43
Myotis myotis 41
Myotis mystacinus 36
Myotis nattereri 39

Nannospalax leucodon 169
Neomys anomalus 21
Neomys fodiens 20
Nyctalus lasiopterus 52
Nyctalus leisleri 50
Nyctalus noctula 51
Nyctereutes procyanoides 66

Odobenus rosmarus 86
Ondatra zibethicus 148
Orca orca 96
Oryctolagus cuniculus 127
Ovibos moschatus 121
Ovis orientalis 126

Peponocephala electra 102
Phoca groenlandica 89
Phoca hispida 88
Phoca vitulina 87
Phocoena phocoena 94
Physeter macrocephalus 105
Pipistrellus kuhlii 48
Pipistrellus nathusii 47
Pipistrellus pipistrellus 46
Pipistrellus savii 49
Pitymys 149
Pitymys bavaricus 149
Pitymys duodecimcostatus 150
Pitymys liechtensteini 149
Pitymys lusitanicus 150
Pitymys savii 151
Pitymys subterraneus 149

Pitymys tatricus 149
Pitymys thomasi 150
Plecotus auritus 57
Plecotus austriacus 58
Procyon lotor 67
Pseudorca crassidens 98
Pteromys volans 136

Rangifer tarandus 119
Rattus norvegicus 164
Rattus rattus 163
Rhinolophis euryale 33
Rhinolophus blasii 35
Rhinolophus ferrumequinum 31
Rhinolophus hipposideros 32
Rhinolophus mehelyi 34
Rousettus aegypticus 30
Rupicapra rupicapra 124

Sciurus carolinus 131
Sciurus vulgaris 130
Sicista betulina 170
Sicista subtilis 171
Sorex alpinus 19
Sorex araneus 17
Sorex caecutiens 16

Sorex isodon 18
Sorex minutissimus 14
Sorex minutus 15
Spalax microphthalmus 168
Spermophilus citellus 134
Spermophilus suslicus 135
Stenella coeruleoabla 100
Steno bredanensis 98
Suncus etruscus 25
Sus scrofa 113

Tadarida teniotis 60
Talpa caeca 28
Talpa europea 27
Talpa romana 29
Talpa stankovici 29
Tamias sibiricus 132
Thalarctos maritimus 69
Tursiops truncatus 97

Ursos arctos 68

Vespertilio murinus 55
Vormela peregusna 76
Vulpes vulpes 65

Ziphius cavirostris 106

The Wildlife Trusts

The Wildlife Trusts are pleased to be associated with these excellent, fully illustrated pocket guide books which provide invaluable information on the wildlife of Britain and Europe. For each book sold, a royalty of 1% of the retail price will be be paid by Dragon's World Ltd to the Royal Society for Nature Conservation, the national office of The Wildlife Trusts (RSNC registered charity no. 207238). This nationwide network of wildlife trusts, urban wildlife groups and Wildlife Watch, the junior branch, is working to protect wildlife in town and country throughout the United Kingdom.

If you would like to find out some more, please contact The Wildlife Trusts, The Green, Witham Park, Waterside South, Lincoln, LN5 7JR.